College Learning

for the *New Global Century*

A REPORT FROM
THE NATIONAL LEADERSHIP COUNCIL FOR

Liberal Education *&* America's Promise

★ ★ ★ ★ ★ ★ ★ ★ ★ ★ ★ ★ ★ ★ ★ ★ ★

Association
of American
Colleges and
Universities

Association
of American
Colleges and
Universities

1818 R Street, NW, Washington, DC 20009

ISBN 978-0-9779210-4-1

The complete text of the LEAP report is available online at www.aacu.org. To order print copies, or
to learn about other AAC&U publications, visit www.aacu.org, e-mail pub_desk@aacu.org, or call
202.387.3760.

*Published with support from the Christian Johnson Endeavor Foundation, the Charles Engelhard Foundation,
Carnegie Corporation of New York, the Andrew W. Mellon Foundation, the Johnson Foundation, AT&T Foundation, Virginia Foundation for the Humanities, and numerous individual donors. The opinions expressed in this report
are those of the authors and do not necessarily reflect those of the funders.*

LEAP

Membership of the National Leadership Council for Liberal Education and America's Promise

"Of all the civil rights for
which the world has
struggled and fought for
5,000 years, the right to
learn is undoubtedly the
most fundamental."
—*W. E. B. DuBois*

Contents

Foreword

★ ★ ★ ★ ★ ★ ★ ★ ★ ★ ★ ★ ★ ★

In 2005, on the occasion of its ninetieth anniversary, the Association of American Colleges and Universities (AAC&U) launched a decade-long initiative, Liberal Education and America's Promise (LEAP): Excellence for Everyone as a Nation Goes to College. AAC&U represents over 1,100 colleges and universities of every type and size: large and small, public and private, research and master's universities, liberal arts colleges, community colleges, and state systems. It is the only major higher education association whose sole focus is the quality of student learning in the college years.

AAC&U launched the LEAP initiative because the academy stands at a crossroads. Millions of students today seek a college education, and record numbers are actually enrolling. Without a serious national effort to recalibrate college learning to the needs of the new global century, however, too few of these students will reap the full benefits of college.

College Learning for the New Global Century, published through the LEAP initiative, spells out the essential aims, learning outcomes, and guiding principles for a twenty-first-century college education. It reports on the promises American society needs to make—and keep—to all who seek a college education and to the society that will depend on graduates' future leadership and capabilities.

The LEAP National Leadership Council comprises educational, business, community, and policy leaders who are strong advocates for educational excellence and change in higher education. These leaders have come together to recommend the essential learning outcomes described in this report because of their own belief in the power of liberal education and its importance in meeting the challenges of the new global century. But they have also been insistent that liberal education cannot be restricted, as it has been in the past, mainly to colleges of arts and sciences, or to the general education courses that most students take in addition to courses in their majors. The essential learning outcomes described in this report apply to the professional and occupational majors as well as the more traditional settings for liberal and liberal arts education.

Each member of the council has already been a vigorous advocate both for educational excellence and for far-reaching change in the way college learning is designed and implemented. Each brought his or her own insight and expertise to the table as this report was being prepared. On behalf of the entire higher education community, we thank them for their wisdom, commitment, and practical advice.

The LEAP report also builds on the work of educators at AAC&U's member campuses and especially those involved since 2000 in AAC&U's Greater Expectations initiative. Through that earlier initiative, AAC&U organized a wide-ranging collaboration with colleges and universities already significantly involved in educational renewal and with many other educational organizations, accrediting groups, state policy makers, higher education executive officers, P–16 leaders, and business and civic leaders. The recommendations in this report are informed and grounded by the many promising examples of educational change identified through these collaborations.

The LEAP Initiative: 2007 and Beyond

The LEAP initiative will continue at least through 2015, the occasion of AAC&U's centennial anniversary. Four discrete but intersecting lines of activity have already been launched. A LEAP Campus Action Network now includes over 150 colleges and universities, as well as numerous partner organizations that are working, in ways appropriate to their mission, to achieve a more empowering liberal education for all today's college students.

LEAP also is working in partnership with leaders in several states, connecting the learning outcomes recommended in this LEAP report with educational priorities for student achievement in those states. In addition, LEAP is both disseminating evidence about student learning outcomes to colleges and universities and providing assistance to colleges and universities about ways to use assessment to deepen student learning.

Finally, LEAP will continue to work, with the National Leadership Council and with AAC&U member presidents across the United States, to champion the value and importance of a twenty-first-century liberal education for all college students.

The United States is faced today with an unprecedented opportunity to provide far more students than ever before with the kind of life-enhancing, liberal—and liberating—education that once was available only to a fortunate few. This nation's future depends on our ability to fulfill the promise of education for all our citizens. In today's knowledge-fueled world, ensuring the most empowering forms of learning for all students should be our top educational priority.

Ronald A. Crutcher
President, Wheaton College (MA)
Cochair, National Leadership Council for
    Liberal Education and America's Promise

Peggy O'Brien
President, Educational Programming,
    Corporation for Public Broadcasting
Cochair, National Leadership Council for
    Liberal Education and America's Promise

Robert Corrigan
President, San Francisco State University
Chair, Board of Directors of the Association
    of American Colleges and Universities

Carol Geary Schneider
President, Association of American Colleges
    and Universities

President's Office

*Association
of American
Colleges and
Universities*

1818 R Street, NW
Washington, DC 20009
202.387.3760
fax: 202.265.9532
www.aacu.org

February 5, 2007

Dear Colleague,

I am pleased to share with you the newly-released report from the National Leadership Council for **Liberal Education and America's Promise (LEAP): Excellence for Everyone as a Nation Goes to College**. LEAP is a ten-year initiative of AAC&U to champion the value of liberal education.

College Learning for the New Global Century spells out the essential aims, learning outcomes, and guiding principles for a twenty-first-century college education. It reports on the promises American society needs to make—and keep—to all who seek a college education and to the society that will depend on graduates' future leadership and capabilities. This report provides a roadmap for reforming higher education and an outline of the key learning outcomes that are essential for a new generation of graduates to succeed in a competitive and complex global environment.

AAC&U released *College Learning for the New Global Century* at a public and press briefing on January 10th and then shared its findings with our members at our recent annual meeting in New Orleans. At both events, AAC&U also released the findings from two national polls conducted in conjunction with the National Leadership Council's preparation of the report. You can find the report summarizing the results of these polls and both the full LEAP report and its Executive Summary online at www.aacu.org/advocacy/leap.

Taken together, the findings from the surveys and the LEAP report affirm that college graduates need more cross-disciplinary knowledge, more skills in a range of areas—especially in the areas of communication, teamwork, and critical thinking and analytic reasoning—and more real-world applications to succeed in a demanding global environment.

There is an emerging consensus, in short, among educators, employers, and recent graduates that colleges need to place more emphasis on these and other key outcomes of a contemporary liberal education.

The LEAP report and related surveys provided needed evidence that liberal education provides the best possible preparation for today's economy, as well as for personal development and civic engagement.

I encourage you to use *College Learning for the New Global Century*—and all of the LEAP publications and meetings AAC&U offers—to help educate constituents about the value of a liberal education in today's world and ensure that all today's students reap the full benefits of this kind of education.

Sincerely,

Carol Geary Schneider
President

**Advancing
Liberal Learning**

Acknowledgments

★ ★ ★ ★ ★ ★ ★ ★ ★ ★ ★ ★ ★ ★

This report is the culmination of more than a year of sustained and collective work by the LEAP National Leadership Council, AAC&U staff members, and numerous advisers throughout the United States. We are especially appreciative of the time and effort council members devoted to the development of this report. Their expertise, wisdom, and commitment were essential in shaping an analysis that reflects the perspectives of educators, employers, and philanthropic and civic leaders.

The LEAP initiative was made possible through a major grant from the Christian Johnson Endeavor Foundation and through complementary funding from many other sources, including the Charles Engelhard Foundation, Carnegie Corporation of New York, the Andrew W. Mellon Foundation, the Johnson Foundation, AT&T Foundation, Virginia Foundation for the Humanities, and numerous individual donors. Particular thanks go to our partners in the several foundations, including Julie J. Kidd, Sally E. Pingree, Daniel F. Fallon, Eugene Tobin, Boyd Gibbons, Carol Johnson, and Robert Vaughan. Their interest and active support have been invaluable. We also thank the many colleges, universities, and partner organizations that have joined us in shaping the LEAP initiative as members of the LEAP Campus Action Network.

Numerous other advisers contributed in significant ways both to this report and to the LEAP initiative. Donald Harward, former president of Bates College and senior fellow at AAC&U, helped spark the entire effort. Special thanks also are due to Ronald Calgaard, W. Robert Connor, Richard Hersh, Stanley Katz, Rebecca Karoff, Lee Knefelkamp, Kevin Reilly, Cora Marrett, Dale Marshall, Richard Morrill, John Nichols, David Paris, Gregory Prince, Robert Shoenberg, and the late Edgar F. Beckham. The AAC&U Board of Directors played a key role both in framing the initiative and in supporting its revisionist views of liberal education. John Casteen, a past member of the AAC&U Board of Directors, also gave active support at crucial points.

Carol Geary Schneider, president of AAC&U and a member of the LEAP National Leadership Council, translated the insights of council members and many other advisers into the analysis and recommendations included in the report. Bethany Zecher Sutton, Ross Miller, Nicole DeMarco, Ursula Gross, and Gretchen Sauvey provided invaluable assistance with research and in coordinating and recording the work of the council. AAC&U Vice Presidents Alma Clayton-Pedersen, Terrel L. Rhodes, and Caryn McTighe Musil contributed insights and editorial assistance.

Members of the AAC&U Office of Communications and Public Affairs and President's Office brought their expertise to the preparation of the report for publication. Special thanks go to Debra Humphreys, Shelley Johnson Carey, Michael Ferguson, and Darbi Bossman for their tireless assistance in planning, editing, design, and production. David Tritelli was the ideal editor, working with dedication to shape the concepts as well as the language. Numerous additional readers reviewed earlier drafts of this report and provided invaluable feedback.

Finally, LEAP builds from AAC&U's earlier initiative, Greater Expectations: The Commitment to Quality as a Nation Goes to College. We gratefully acknowledge the thousands of campus leaders who contributed to that work, and especially its key leaders: Andrea Leskes, now president of the Institute for American Universities, and Judith Ramaley, now president of Winona State University.

Executive Highlights

★ ★ ★ ★ ★ ★ ★ ★ ★ ★ ★ ★ ★ ★ ★ ★

College Learning for the New Global Century is a report about the aims and outcomes of a twenty-first-century college education. It is also a report about the promises we need to make—and keep—to all students who aspire to a college education, especially to those for whom college is a route, perhaps the only possible route, to a better future.

With college education more important than ever before, both to individual opportunity and to American prosperity, policy attention has turned to a new set of priorities: the expansion of access, the reduction of costs, and accountability for student success.

These issues are important, but something equally important has been left off the table.

Across all the discussion of access, affordability, and even accountability, there has been a near-total public and policy silence about what contemporary college graduates need to know and be able to do.

This report fills that void. It builds from the recognition, already widely shared, that in a demanding economic and international environment, Americans will need further learning beyond high school.

The National Leadership Council for Liberal Education and America's Promise believes that the policy commitment to expanded college access must be anchored in an equally strong commitment to educational excellence. Student success in college cannot be documented—as it usually is—only in terms of enrollment, persistence, and degree attainment. These widely used metrics, while important, miss entirely the question of whether students who have placed their hopes for the future in higher education are actually achieving the kind of learning they need for a complex and volatile world.

In the twenty-first century, the world itself is setting very high expectations for knowledge and skill. This report—based on extensive input both from educators and employers—responds to these new global challenges. It describes the learning contemporary students need from college, and what it will take to help them achieve it.

> "Student success in college cannot be documented—as it usually is—only in terms of enrollment, persistence, and degree attainment."

Preparing Students for Twenty-First-Century Realities

In recent years, the ground has shifted for Americans in virtually every important sphere of life—economic, global, cross-cultural, environ-

> *"The policy commitment to expanded college access must be anchored in an equally strong commitment to educational excellence."*

mental, civic. The world is being dramatically reshaped by scientific and technological innovations, global interdependence, cross-cultural encounters, and changes in the balance of economic and political power.

These waves of dislocating change will only intensify. The context in which today's students will make choices and compose lives is one of disruption rather than certainty, and of interdependence rather than insularity. This volatility also applies to careers. Studies show that Americans already change jobs ten times in the two decades after they turn eighteen, with such change even more frequent for younger workers.

Taking stock of these developments, educators and employers have begun to reach similar conclusions—an emerging consensus—about the kinds of learning Americans need from college. The recommendations in this report are informed by the views of employers, by new standards in a number of the professions, and by a multiyear dialogue with hundreds of colleges, community colleges, and universities about the aims and best practices for a twenty-first-century education.

The goal of this report is to move from off-camera analysis to public priorities and action.

What Matters in College?

American college students already know that they want a degree. The challenge is to help students become highly intentional about the forms of learning and accomplishment that the degree should represent.

The LEAP National Leadership Council calls on American society to give new priority to a set of educational outcomes that all students need from higher learning, outcomes that are closely calibrated with the challenges of a complex and volatile world.

Keyed to work, life, and citizenship, the essential learning outcomes recommended in this report are important for all students and should be fostered and developed across the entire educational experience, and in the context of students' major fields. They provide a new framework to guide students' cumulative progress—as well as curricular alignment—from school through college.

The LEAP National Leadership Council does not call for a "one-size-fits-all" curriculum. The recommended learning outcomes can and should be achieved through many different programs of study and in all collegiate institutions, including colleges, community colleges and technical institutes, and universities, both public and private.

THE ESSENTIAL LEARNING OUTCOMES

Beginning in school, and continuing at successively higher levels across their college studies, students should prepare for twenty-first-century challenges by gaining:

KNOWLEDGE OF HUMAN CULTURES AND THE PHYSICAL AND NATURAL WORLD

- Through study in the sciences and mathematics, social sciences, humanities, histories, languages, and the arts

Focused by engagement with big questions, both contemporary and enduring

INTELLECTUAL AND PRACTICAL SKILLS, INCLUDING

- Inquiry and analysis
- Critical and creative thinking
- Written and oral communication
- Quantitative literacy
- Information literacy
- Teamwork and problem solving

Practiced extensively, across the curriculum, in the context of progressively more challenging problems, projects, and standards for performance

PERSONAL AND SOCIAL RESPONSIBILITY, INCLUDING

- Civic knowledge and engagement—local and global
- Intercultural knowledge and competence
- Ethical reasoning and action
- Foundations and skills for lifelong learning

Anchored through active involvement with diverse communities and real-world challenges

INTEGRATIVE LEARNING, INCLUDING

- Synthesis and advanced accomplishment across general and specialized studies

Demonstrated through the application of knowledge, skills, and responsibilities to new settings and complex problems

"The essential learning outcomes provide a new framework to guide students' cumulative progress from school through college."

Liberal Education and American Capability

Reflecting the traditions of American higher education since the founding, the term "liberal education" headlines the kinds of learning needed for a free society and for the full development of human talent. Liberal education has always been this nation's signature educational tradition, and this report builds on its core values: expanding horizons, building understanding of the wider world, honing analytical and communication skills, and fostering responsibilities beyond self.

However, in a deliberate break with the academic categories developed in the twentieth century, the LEAP National Leadership Council disputes the idea that liberal education is achieved only through studies in arts and sciences disciplines. It also challenges the conventional view that liberal education is, by definition, "nonvocational."

The council defines liberal education for the twenty-first century as a comprehensive set of aims and outcomes that are essential for all students because they are important to all fields of endeavor. Today, in an economy that is dependent on innovation and global savvy, these outcomes have become the keys to economic vitality and individual opportunity. They are the foundations for American success in all fields—from technology and the sciences to communications and the creative arts.

The LEAP National Leadership Council recommends, therefore, that the essential aims and outcomes be emphasized across every field of college study, whether the field is conventionally considered one of the arts and sciences disciplines or whether it is one of the professional and technical fields (business, engineering, education, health, the performing arts, etc.) in which the majority of college students currently major. General education plays a role, but it is not possible to squeeze all these important aims into the general education program alone. The majors must address them as well.

A New Framework for Excellence

The LEAP National Leadership Council recommends, in sum, an education that intentionally fosters, across multiple fields of study, wide-ranging knowledge of science, cultures, and society; high-level intellectual and practical skills; an active commitment to personal and social responsibility; and the demonstrated ability to apply learning to complex problems and challenges.

The council further calls on educators to help students become "intentional learners" who focus, across ascending levels of study and diverse academic programs, on achieving the essential learning outcomes. But to help students do this, educational communities will also have to become far more intentional themselves—both about the kinds of learning students need, and about effective educational practices that help students learn to integrate and apply their learning.

In a society as diverse as the United States, there can be no "one-size-fits-all" design for learning that serves all students and all areas of study. The diversity that characterizes American higher education remains a source of vitality and strength.

Yet all educational institutions and all fields of study also share in a common obligation to prepare their graduates as fully as possible for the real-world demands of work, citizenship, and life in a complex and fast-changing society. In this context, there is great value in a broadly defined educational framework that provides both a shared sense of the aims of education and strong emphasis on effective practices that help students achieve these aims.

To highlight these shared responsibilities, the council urges a new compact, between educators and American society, to adopt and achieve new Principles of Excellence (see p. 26).

Informed by a generation of innovation and by scholarly research on effective practices in teaching, learning, and curriculum, the Principles of Excellence offer both challenging standards and flexible guidance for an era of educational reform and renewal.

Taken together, the Principles of Excellence underscore the need to teach students how to integrate and apply their learning—across multiple levels of schooling and across disparate fields of study. The principles call for a far-reaching shift in the focus of schooling from accumulating course credits to building real-world capabilities.

A Time for Leadership and Action

The Principles of Excellence build from a generation of innovation that is already well under way. As higher education has reached out to serve an ever wider and more diverse set of students, there has been widespread experimentation to develop more effective educational practices and to determine "what works" with today's college students.

Some of these innovations are so well established that research is already emerging about their effectiveness. This report provides a guide to tested and effective educational practices (see appendix A).

To date, however, these active and engaged forms of learning have served only a fraction of students. New research suggests that the benefits are especially significant for students who start farther behind. But often, these students are not the ones actually participating in the high-impact practices.

With campus experimentation already well advanced—on every one of the Principles of Excellence—it is time to move from "pilot efforts" to more comprehensive commitments. The United States comprehensively transformed its designs for learning, at all levels, in the late nineteenth and early twentieth centuries. Now, as we enter the new global century, Americans need to mobilize again to advance a contemporary set of goals, guiding principles, and practices that will prepare all college students—not just the fortunate few—for twenty-first-century realities.

What will it take?

As a community, we should

- make the essential learning outcomes and the Principles of Excellence priorities on campus;
- form coalitions, across sectors, to advance all students' long-term interests;
- build principled and determined leadership, including
  - high-profile advocacy from presidents, trustees, school leaders, and employers
  - curricular leadership from knowledgeable scholars and teachers
  - policy leadership at multiple levels to support and reward a new framework for educational excellence;
- put employers in direct dialogue with students;
- reclaim the connections between liberal education and democratic freedom.

While recognized leaders can make higher achievement a priority, faculty and teachers who work directly with students are the only

"American education calls for a far-reaching shift in the focus of schooling from accumulating course credits to building real-world capabilities."

ones who can make it actually happen. At all levels—nationally, regionally, and locally—they will need to take the lead in developing guidelines, curricula, and assignments that connect rich content with students' progressive mastery of essential skills and capabilities. Equally important, those responsible for educating future teachers and future faculty must work to ensure that they are well prepared to help students achieve the intended learning.

Liberal Education and America's Promise

With this report, the LEAP National Leadership Council urges a comprehensive commitment, not just to prepare all students for college, but to provide the most powerful forms of learning for all who enroll in college.

Working together, with determination, creativity, and a larger sense of purpose, Americans can fulfill the promise of a liberating college education—for every student and for America's future.

INTRODUCTION
A Dangerous Silence

★ ★ ★ ★ ★ ★ ★ ★ ★ ★ ★ ★ ★ ★ ★ ★ ★

This is a pivotal moment for higher education, a time when we must work together for the kind of learning graduates need for an interdependent and volatile world. And it is also a precarious moment when short-sighted educational choices may prove permanently limiting to Americans' prospects.

Americans have long placed great value on higher education, but for most of our history, a college education was a privilege reserved only for the few. Today, that situation has changed fundamentally. Far-reaching global, economic, and technological developments have converged to make postsecondary learning an imperative for almost everyone. Both this country's future economic growth and individual opportunity are now closely tied to the attainment of high levels of knowledge and skill, and to the ability to continue learning over a lifetime.

Responding to this new environment, 75 percent of high school graduates already are enrolling in college within two years of graduation;[1] 67 percent of students matriculate immediately after completing high school.[2] An even higher number—94 percent of current high school students—say they want to attend college after high school.[3]

Policy leaders also are responding. Reading the numbers, they see the jarring disconnect between aspiration and actual achievement. Of students who begin high school at age fourteen, fewer than three in ten will hold a baccalaureate degree twelve years later, while one in five will still not have finished high school.[4] At the same time, both college enrollment and degree attainment remain stubbornly stratified by income and race.[5] And so there is new pressure to expand college access, especially for those from low-income backgrounds; strengthen college preparation for all students; make higher education more affordable; and increase graduation rates. In 2005, the federal government gave added impetus to these policy priorities by forming the Commission on the Future of Higher Education and charging it to propose new directions for access, affordability, and accountability.[6]

Stunningly, however, American society has yet to confront the most basic and far-reaching question of all. Across all the work on access, readiness, costs, and even accountability, there has been a near-total public silence about what contemporary college graduates need to know and be able to do.

> "There has been a near-total public silence about what contemporary college graduates need to know and be able to do."

FIGURE 1

FINDINGS ON SELECTED LIBERAL EDUCATION OUTCOMES

Math
- Eight percent of college seniors are "proficient" at level 3 math, up from 5 percent of freshmen

Writing
- Eleven percent of college seniors are "proficient" at level 3 writing

Critical Thinking
- Six percent of college seniors are "proficient" in critical thinking, 77 percent are "not proficient"

Global Knowledge and Skills
- Less than 13 percent of college students achieve basic competence in a language other than English
- Less than 34 percent of college students earn credit for an international studies class; of those who do, only 13 percent take more than four classes
- Less than 10 percent of college students participate in study abroad programs
- Between 5 and 10 percent of college students achieve basic competence in a language other than English, take more than four international studies classes, and participate in study abroad programs

Sources: Academic Profile, Educational Testing Service (2003–04); Clifford Adelman, "'Global Preparedness' of Pre-9/11 College Graduates: What the U.S. Longitudinal Studies Say," *Tertiary Education and Management* 10 (2004): 243.

Yet off the public radar screen, evidence is mounting that Americans can no longer afford to ignore these questions (see fig. 1).

Former Harvard University President Derek Bok has summarized a wealth of separate studies on student learning in his 2006 book, *Our Underachieving Colleges*.[7] As he reports, college students are underperforming in virtually every area of academic endeavor, from essential intellectual skills such as critical thinking, writing, and quantitative reasoning to public purposes such as civic engagement and ethical learning. Other research concludes that less than 10 percent of today's college graduates have the knowledge and experience to make them globally prepared.[8] Confirming this portrait of underachievement, less than 25 percent of human resource professionals report that the recent college graduates they employ are well prepared for the workforce.[9]

Genuinely alarmed by their own international scanning, business leaders have added another compelling layer of critique. In one urgent report after another,[10] they warn about Americans' dangerous loss of comparative advantage in the so-called STEM disciplines: science, technology, engineering, and mathematics (see fig. 2). And this, they point out, will inevitably mean a loss of economic advantage as well.

Elementary and secondary schools play a big role in this pattern of underachievement,[11] and calls are mounting for "new alignment" between high school and college curricula. But there is no set of overarching goals for students' cumulative learning that can reliably guide educational reform and strengthen student accomplishment from school through higher education. In the absence of such goals, two systems—each in need of significant change—are being patched awkwardly together.

In principle, policy efforts to develop new forms of accountability for higher education would seem to require an answer to the question of what college students need to learn. In practice, that question has been avoided. Leaders in many states, as well as members of the federal Commission on the Future of Higher Education, have urged that states and colleges adopt standardized testing as a way to spur educational reform. But none of the policy efforts has provided an answer to the most basic question: what do students need to know?

This public silence about what matters in college is dangerous.

To students, it can send the self-defeating message that the diploma itself—rather than the quality of learning it represents—is the key to the future. Many students, in fact, speak of college in just that way, and they view the degree as a ticket to be stamped before they can move forward. "It's just a piece of paper. But that piece of paper will get you the interview at whatever job you want."[12]

Contemporary students need and deserve better guidance. The majority no longer follow a traditional path through college. Nearly 60 percent of those who earn a baccalaureate degree now enroll in two or more institutions before they finish their studies.[13] Most students work, many attend part-time, and since 40 percent are twenty-four or older, many are raising families as well.[14] These trends will accelerate as higher education reaches out with new vigor to increase college access for those who have historically been underserved: low-income students and racial and ethnic minorities. In a demanding world, a first-rate education is plainly more important than ever. But today's students need greater clarity about the meaning of that goal as they move across multiple colleges and universities on what is often an extended journey toward a degree.

To faculty and staff, countless numbers of whom are already working to reverse the pattern of underachievement in college, the public silence about what matters in college is discouraging, even demoralizing. There have been widespread efforts throughout higher education for over a generation to design and advance new forms of active and engaged learning—practices that ask students to apply their learning to complex, unscripted problems and projects. There is mounting evidence that some of these innovations in teaching and learning can now be described as "effective educational practices" (see appendix A) because they result in higher levels of achievement.[15] The benefits are especially striking for minority and low-income students.[16] But the public—including college-bound students—knows almost nothing about these emerging innovations. Moreover, with funds for expanding the reach of such reforms in sparse supply, these effective educational practices still serve only a fraction of today's college students—with the students who could benefit most still losing out.

To markets, the silence about what matters in college has already sent the strong message that, if you just call it "college," anything goes. The label now applies to every possible form of postsecondary activity, from campuses where faculty engage even first-year students with the emerging frontiers of knowledge to the more than four thousand commercial or "career" colleges whose mission is to prepare students only for a specific occupation (see appendix B). Policy leaders often recommend career colleges as an efficient way to expand access for students who, in an earlier era, would not have attended college at all. With Congressional blessing, these institutions are now eligible for tax-supported student aid dollars.

While there is certainly a value in targeted training, students and the general public deserve help in seeing the difference between a comprehensive college education—whether at a community college or a university—and a program designed to provide a much more limited form of preparation. School reformers are currently working all over the United States to dismantle the inequitable systems of academic versus vocational "tracking" that became common in American high schools during the twentieth century and to replace them with a rigorous preparatory curriculum for all high school students. Yet differential tracks of the same kind are multiplying in postsecondary education. In higher education, as in the high schools, these tracks are stratified by income and race.

The LEAP National Leadership Council strongly supports current efforts throughout American society to expand college access and degree attainment, especially for students from underserved communities (see fig. 3). The analysis and recommendations presented in this

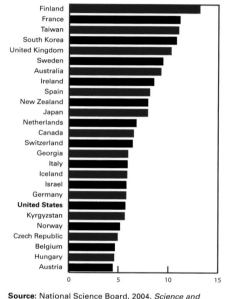

FIGURE 2

SCIENCE AND ENGINEERING DEGREE ATTAINMENT BY COUNTRY

Percentage of twenty-four-year-olds with first university degrees in natural sciences or engineering, 2000 or most recent year

Source: National Science Board, 2004. *Science and Engineering Indicators 2004*. Two volumes, Arlington, VA; National Science Foundation (volume 1, NSB, 04-1; volume 2: NSB 04-1A). Appendix Table 2-35.

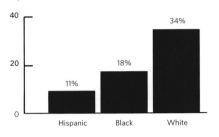
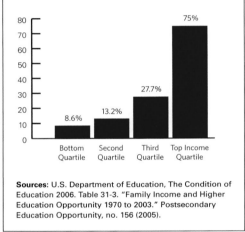
report draw extensively on a generation of experimentation that was spurred in large part by the need to educate these recently arrived students far more effectively.

But the commitment to expanded college access needs to be anchored in an equally strong commitment to educational excellence. Student success in college cannot be defined only in terms of enrollment, persistence, and degree completion. These metrics, while important, miss entirely the question of whether students who have placed their hopes for the future in higher education are actually achieving the kind of learning they need.

The public and policy inattention to the aims, scope, and level of student learning in college threatens to erode the potential value of college enrollment for many American students.

College Learning for the New Global Century is a report about the aims and outcomes of a twenty-first-century college education. It is also a report about the promises American society needs to make—and keep—to all college students, especially those for whom college is a route, perhaps the only possible route, to the American dream.

PART 1
What Matters in College?

★ ★ ★ ★ ★ ★ ★ ★ ★ ★ ★ ★ ★ ★ ★ ★ ★

In releasing this report, the National Leadership Council for Liberal Education and America's Promise breaks the prevailing silence on the important aims and outcomes of a twenty-first-century college education. *College Learning for the New Global Century* calls on American society to give new priority to a set of educational outcomes that all students need from higher learning—outcomes that are closely calibrated with the realities of our complex and volatile world.

The council urges a new recognition that, in this global century, every student—not just the fortunate few—will need wide-ranging and cross-disciplinary knowledge, higher-level skills, an active sense of personal and social responsibility, and a demonstrated ability to apply knowledge to complex problems. The learning students need is best described as a liberal—and liberating—education.

In a deliberate break with the academic categories developed in the last century, liberal education is defined in this report not as a discrete set of disciplines—the "liberal arts and sciences" alone—but rather as a comprehensive set of aims and outcomes that are essential both for a globally engaged democracy and for a dynamic, innovation-fueled economy (see p. 12). Reflecting the traditions of American higher education since the founding, the term "liberal education" is not used in any partisan sense, but rather as a description of the kinds of learning needed to sustain a free society and to enable the full development of human talent.

The educational aims and outcomes recommended here are needed in every area of human endeavor. These outcomes can and will be achieved in many different ways, across highly diverse institutional contexts and fields of study. But the forms of learning depicted on page 12 are important for all students and should be fostered across the entire educational experience.

Further, this report calls on policy leaders to expand substantially the investment in active, hands-on, collaborative, and inquiry-based forms of teaching and learning—making full use of new educational technologies—to ensure that all students have rich opportunities to fully achieve the intended learning outcomes. The use of effective and engaging educational practices will be the key to higher achievement for contemporary college students.

> "The educational aims and outcomes recommended here are needed in every area of human endeavor."

The Essential Learning Outcomes

★ ★ ★ ★ ★ ★ ★ ★ ★ ★ ★ ★ ★ ★ ★ ★ ★ ★ ★ ★

Beginning in school, and continuing at successively higher levels across their college studies, students should prepare for twenty-first-century challenges by gaining:

✦ Knowledge of Human Cultures and the Physical and Natural World

- Through study in the sciences and mathematics, social sciences, humanities, histories, languages, and the arts

Focused *by engagement with big questions, both contemporary and enduring*

✦ Intellectual and Practical Skills, including

- Inquiry and analysis
- Critical and creative thinking
- Written and oral communication
- Quantitative literacy
- Information literacy
- Teamwork and problem solving

Practiced extensively, *across the curriculum, in the context of progressively more challenging problems, projects, and standards for performance*

✦ Personal and Social Responsibility, including

- Civic knowledge and engagement—local and global
- Intercultural knowledge and competence
- Ethical reasoning and action
- Foundations and skills for lifelong learning

Anchored *through active involvement with diverse communities and real-world challenges*

✦ Integrative Learning, including

- Synthesis and advanced accomplishment across general and specialized studies

Demonstrated *through the application of knowledge, skills, and responsibilities to new settings and complex problems*

Note: This listing was developed through a multiyear dialogue with hundreds of colleges and universities about needed goals for student learning; analysis of a long series of recommendations and reports from the business community; and analysis of the accreditation requirements for engineering, business, nursing, and teacher education. The findings are documented in previous publications of the Association of American Colleges and Universities: *Greater Expectations: A New Vision for Learning as a Nation Goes to College* (2002), *Taking Responsibility for the Quality of the Baccalaureate Degree* (2004), and *Liberal Education Outcomes: A Preliminary Report on Achievement in College* (2005).

LEAP

The essential learning outcomes recommended in this report reflect an important emerging consensus—among educators *and* employers—about the kinds of learning needed for a complex and volatile world. This new consensus reflects a dawning awareness that America's future will depend on an unprecedented determination to develop human talent as broadly and fully as possible:

- **In an era when knowledge is the key to the future**, all students need the scope and depth of learning that will enable them to understand and navigate the dramatic forces—physical, cultural, economic, technological—that directly affect the quality, character, and perils of the world in which they live.

- **In an economy where every industry—from the trades to advanced technology enterprises—is challenged to innovate or be displaced**, all students need the kind of intellectual skills and capacities that enable them to get things done in the world, at a high level of effectiveness.

- **In a democracy that is diverse, globally engaged, and dependent on citizen responsibility**, all students need an informed concern for the larger good because nothing less will renew our fractured and diminished commons.

- **In a world of daunting complexity**, all students need practice in integrating and applying their learning to challenging questions and real-world problems.

- **In a period of relentless change**, all students need the kind of education that leads them to ask not just "how do we get this done?" but also "what is most worth doing?"

With organizations constantly reinventing their products and their processes, and with questions about public and life choices more complex than ever, the world itself is setting higher expectations for knowledge and skill. The essential learning outcomes respond to this reality.

Liberal Education and American Capability

In 1947, the Truman Commission on Higher Education assigned liberal education to general education courses taken in the first two years of college. Its report provided federal sanction for the view that liberal/general education addresses the "nonvocational" aspects of learning.[17] That view has been widely influential. On many four-year campuses and at most community colleges, liberal education is now virtually synonymous with general education: broad courses that students usually take in the initial phase of college, before focusing on a major.

Research confirms that, in the wider society, many still see liberal education as the "nonvocational" or "less marketable" part of the curriculum.[18] That twentieth-century view is now obsolete, and this report presents a very different vision for college learning.

In an economy fueled by innovation, the capabilities developed through a liberal education have become America's most valuable

"In an economy fueled by innovation, the capabilities developed through a liberal education have become America's most valuable economic asset."

"These outcomes can and should be addressed in different ways across varied fields of study."

economic asset. The student learning outcomes recommended on page 12—rich knowledge, higher-level skills and creativity, social responsibility, examined values, and the ability to apply learning to complex and unscripted problems—are the keys to America's promise. These forms of learning are now needed in every part of life, including the workplace, and in all fields of study, including the professional and occupational fields. Because of their importance, these outcomes are concerns for the entire educational experience, and not just for the first two years of college. The aims and outcomes of a liberal education are essential to our nation's future.

These essential learning outcomes should become the guiding compass for student accomplishment in the twenty-first century. They provide a common framework both for new forms of accountability and for new and more productive educational alignments between high school and college. The outcomes also serve as a compass to help students connect general education and college majors.

These outcomes can and should be addressed in different ways across varied fields of study. Engineers, for example, use quite different inquiry and communication skills than anthropologists. Intercultural preparation will mean one thing for an elementary school teacher and another for a graduate heading into global business. Even effective writing takes different forms in different fields and settings. Because competence is always related to context, students need to work on the liberal education outcomes in their major field(s) as well as their precollegiate and general studies. This report does not recommend teaching "skills" apart from content and context.

This report *is* a call to ensure that students have every opportunity to really develop these essential capabilities, whatever they study and wherever they go to college.

The essential learning outcomes describe capacities that will be important to each student's future and to the vitality of our society. They provide a shared direction and framework for the entire continuum of learning, from school through college, and beyond.

College Learning for the New Global Century elaborates this vision for a twenty-first-century college education and recommends a course of action to achieve it.

PART 2

From the American Century to the Global Century

★ ★ ★ ★ ★ ★ ★ ★ ★ ★ ★ ★ ★ ★ ★ ★ ★

In recent years, the ground has shifted for Americans in virtually every important sphere of life—economic, global, cross-cultural, environmental, civic. The world around us is being dramatically reshaped by scientific and technological innovations, global interdependence, cross-cultural encounters, and changes in the balance of economic and political power. Only a few years ago, Americans envisioned a future in which this nation would be the world's only superpower. Today it is clear that the United States—and individual Americans—will be challenged to engage in unprecedented ways with the global community, collaboratively and competitively.

These seismic waves of dislocating change will only intensify. The world in which today's students will make choices and compose lives is one of disruption rather than certainty, and of interdependence rather than insularity. To succeed in a chaotic environment, graduates will need to be intellectually resilient, cross-culturally and scientifically literate, technologically adept, ethically anchored, and fully prepared for a future of continuous and cross-disciplinary learning. Learning about cultures and social structures dramatically different from one's own is no longer a matter just for specialists. Intercultural learning is already one of the new basics in a contemporary liberal education, because it is essential for work, civil society, and social life. Scientific and technological learning are equally fundamental and may well determine the difference between those who are prepared to deal with change and those who are buffeted by it.

Narrow Learning Is Not Enough

The general public—and many college students—continue to believe that choosing a "marketable" college major is the key to future economic opportunity. Guided by this conviction, many students see study in their major field as the main point of college, and actively resist academic requirements that push them toward a broader education. Many policy makers hold a similar view of career preparation, evidenced by their support for occupational colleges and programs that promise initial job readiness but not much else.

Those who endorse narrow learning are blind to the realities of the new global economy. Careers themselves have become volatile.

"The world in which today's students will make choices and compose lives is one of disruption rather than certainty, and of interdependence rather than insularity."

"Using a business rather than an academic vocabulary, employers are urging more—and better—liberal education, not less."

Studies already show that Americans change jobs ten times in the two decades following college, with such changes even more frequent for younger workers.[19] Moreover, employers are calling with new urgency for graduates who are broadly prepared and who also possess the analytical and practical skills that are essential both for innovation and for organizational effectiveness:

- "Employers do not want, and have not advocated for, students prepared for narrow workforce specialties. . . . Virtually all occupational endeavors require a working appreciation of the historical, cultural, ethical, and global environments that surround the application of skilled work." (Roberts T. Jones, president, Education Workforce Policy, LLC)[20]

- "Intel Corp. Chairman Craig Barrett has said that 90 percent of the products his company delivers on the final day of each year did not exist on the first day of the same year. To succeed in that kind of marketplace, U.S. firms need employees who are flexible, knowledgeable, and scientifically and mathematically literate." (Norman R. Augustine, retired chairman and chief executive of Lockheed Martin Corporation)[21]

- "[The] curriculum needs to help students develop . . . leadership, teamwork, problem solving, time management, communication and analytical thinking." (Business–Higher Education Forum)[22]

- "[Business leaders are] frustrated with their inability to find '360 degree people'. . . ." (Findings from 2006 focus groups among business executives)[23]

- "Integrated capabilities are the key to this industry's future." (Keith Peden, senior vice president of human resources, Raytheon Company, 2006)[24]

Using a business rather than an academic vocabulary, employers are urging more—and better—liberal education, not less. Because employers view innovation as their most important comparative advantage, they seek to hire graduates who can think beyond the routine, and who have the ability not just to adapt to change, but to help create it.

Responding to employer concerns, the engineering community is already pioneering the approach to a twenty-first-century liberal education recommended in this report. The engineers' goal is to graduate what some are calling "T-shaped students," with the vertical part of the "T" representing the traditional parts of an engineering degree, and the crossbar pointing to competencies traditionally identified with the "liberal arts"—including ethics, global knowledge, intercultural literacy, and strong communication and collaborative skills (see fig. 4). The "T" itself shows that these different capabilities need to be *integrated* so that students can apply them in work and community settings.

Humanists may see similar potential in the letter "H," where the crossbar represents field-specific knowledge and skills and the vertical bars represent capacities related to context and community. Whatever the model, the message to students is the same. Employers do not want "toothpick" graduates who have learned only the technical skills and who arrive in the workplace deep but narrow. These workers are sidelined early on, employers report, because they cannot break out of their mental cubicles.[25]

Broad capabilities and perspectives are now important in all fields, from the sciences to business to the humanities. The new economic reality is that narrow preparation in a single area—whether that field is chemistry or information technology or history—is exactly the opposite of what graduates need from college. Study-in-depth remains an important part of the overall pattern for college learning. But students deserve to know that focusing only on one specialty is far from enough.

By now, readers who value liberal education may be actively protesting: it's not just about the economy! And we agree. The aims and benefits of liberal education go far beyond work to enrich every sphere of life—environmental, civic, cultural, imaginative, ethical. These important topics are addressed in later pages.

But this report places special emphasis on liberal education as the portal to economic opportunity because so much of the public—and so many students—have been told just the opposite. Today, powerful social forces, reinforced by public policies, pull students—especially first-generation and adult students—toward a narrowly instrumental approach to college. This report urges educators to resist and reverse that downward course. It is time to guide students away from limiting choices and toward a contemporary understanding of what matters in college.

The way forward is to make a new commitment to provide a horizon-expanding liberal education for all college students, not just for some. Through much of the twentieth century, liberal education was identified only with selected academic fields—the arts and sciences—and, more recently, with the most selective colleges and universities.[26] The net effect has been to position liberal education as an elite option, the expected form of learning at The University of Chicago, Pomona College, or the University of Virginia—and in all campus honors programs—but hardly necessary for everyone.

In this new global century, these older views stand in the way of needed change. Liberal education has been America's premier educational tradition since the founding, and the recommendations in this report build on its core strengths: broad knowledge, strong intellectual skills, personal and social responsibility. But in a democratic society, the goal must be to extend opportunity and excellence to everyone, and not just to a fortunate minority.

The way to achieve this goal is to make the essential learning outcomes a shared priority for all students, whatever their chosen areas of study, and wherever they enroll in college.

The World Is Changing and Liberal Education Must Change Too

This report recommends, in sum, a challenging and liberating education that develops essential capacities, engages significant questions—both contemporary and enduring—in science and society, and connects

"This report places special emphasis on liberal education as the portal to economic opportunity because so much of the public—and so many students—have been told just the opposite."

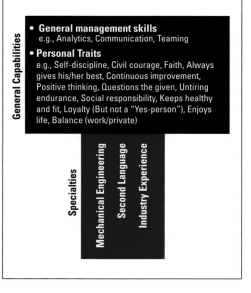

FIGURE 4

WHAT SIEMENS ADVISES FOR SUCCESS: BUILD A T-SHAPED PROFILE

General Capabilities

• **General management skills**
e.g., Analytics, Communication, Teaming

• **Personal Traits**
e.g., Self-discipline, Civil courage, Faith, Always gives his/her best, Continuous improvement, Positive thinking, Questions the given, Untiring endurance, Social responsibility, Keeps healthy and fit, Loyalty (But not a "Yes-person"), Enjoys life, Balance (work/private)

Specialties

Mechanical Engineering
Second Language
Industry Experience

FIGURE 5

REMAPPING LIBERAL EDUCATION

	Liberal Education in the Twentieth Century	Liberal Education in the Twenty-first Century
What	• an elite curriculum • nonvocational • an option for the fortunate	• a necessity for all students • essential for success in a global economy and for informed citizenship
Where	• liberal arts colleges or colleges of arts and sciences in larger institutions	• all schools, community colleges, colleges, and universities; across all fields of study (recommended)
How	• through studies in arts and sciences fields ("the major") and/or through general education in the initial years of college	• through studies across the entire educational continuum: school through college (recommended)

"In a democratic society, the goal must be to extend opportunity and excellence to everyone, and not just to a fortunate minority."

analytical skills with practical experience in putting knowledge to use.

In doing so, this report also calls on educators to adapt liberal education to the needs of our time. Certain aims of liberal education are enduring through every era, to be sure. Helping students master the arts of inquiry, analysis, and communication is the signature strength of a liberal education and a core reason why it is the best and most powerful preparation both for the economy and for democracy.

But the key to continued national vitality is the ability of citizens to adapt creatively to new challenges. Liberal education in the United States did transform its practices, dramatically, just a century ago. Starting about 1870 and continuing into the next century, the rise of new disciplines and a new role for the United States in the world led to revolutionary change in the organization of the undergraduate curriculum. A comparably dramatic change in the approach to liberal education is needed today to better prepare college graduates for the complex realities of this new global century (see fig. 5).

The first step toward a contemporary approach to liberal education is to remap the educational landscape so that all parts of the academy and all fields of study address—in ways appropriate to their subjects—the essential learning outcomes recommended in part 1 (see p. 12).

To take this step, higher education will also need to break out of the academic categories and silos that were established in the last curriculum revolution, and that still organize the division of labor across most campuses, from community colleges to research universities.

As a result of the last curricular revolution, liberal or liberal arts education is conventionally defined as study in selected academic fields: the humanities, the social sciences, the sciences, and, by the last quarter of the twentieth century, the arts as well. The many professional and applied fields—including engineering, business, education, and health—have not traditionally been seen as part of a liberal education.

The resulting lines of demarcation guide students' educational choices to this day on thousands of campuses. Because of these inherited dividing lines, millions of college students are routinely compelled to choose *either* a liberal arts and sciences pathway *or* a professional pathway just to fill out their college applications. The message sent by this forced choice is exactly the opposite of what students need to know.

The traditional boundaries between the liberal arts and the professional fields are not just a bureaucratic inconvenience. In practice, they have created academic silos that impede faculty and staff efforts to foster a more holistic and integrative approach to college learning. It is in everyone's interest to create new crosswalks and communal spaces that support educational collaboration across the traditional academic dividing lines between the liberal arts and sciences and the professional fields. But if collaborations are to succeed, they need to be based in shared goals. The essential learning outcomes, which place strong emphasis on teaching students to integrate and apply their learning, provide this larger sense of shared interests.

Within this altered educational landscape, many different pathways to a liberal education are possible. Students will continue to be able to choose among a variety of educational settings: universities, colleges, community colleges, faith-based institutions, technical institutes. Students will still concentrate in selected fields because, while not sufficient, studies in depth are important. They will certainly need a rich mix of arts and sciences courses in order to learn about the wider world. **The key change is that, whatever and wherever they elect to study, each college student will be helped to achieve, in ways appropriate to his or her educational interests, a high level of integrative learning and demonstrated accomplishment across the full range of essential learning outcomes.**

Movement toward this needed remapping has already begun. The long-standing boundaries between the professional fields and the arts and sciences have started to blur. Engineering and technology fields have forged the way. The Accrediting Board for Engineering and Technology now looks for evidence that programs are teaching students to integrate their liberal arts competencies with their technical studies.[27] Similar developments are emerging across many professional fields, and on many campuses.

Simultaneously, many arts and sciences departments are placing new emphasis on "practical experience" and "applied learning" through internships, service learning, student projects, and community-based research. Many campuses also are inventing a "vertical" or four-year framework for general education, with the explicit goal of fostering new connections between students' specialized studies and their broader learning about science, cultures, and society.

Students themselves are adding to this remapping by choosing double majors or majors and minors that freely span the "liberal arts/professional" divide.

These forward steps notwithstanding, many of the most imaginative efforts to forge new connections between the liberal arts and sciences and professional studies still hover on the margins. Higher education needs new leadership and new determination to move these promising developments from the margins to the center.

Engaging Twenty-First-Century Realities

Breaking out of the academic silos is a good beginning, but much more needs to be done in order to align teaching and learning practices with the realities of the new global century. In the twentieth century, both school and college studies were organized, reflecting the sensibilities of the industrial age, in terms of modular parts: disciplines, subjects, courses, credit hours. But this modular curriculum, organized a century ago and still largely intact, has become increasingly dysfunctional. The disciplines are taught as ends in themselves, and so too are most courses. Yet students are taking courses in many different disciplines, and often at two or more institutions. For many, the result is a fragmented and incoherent educational experience rather than steady progress toward deeper and more integrated understandings and capacities.

"Because of these inherited dividing lines, millions of college students are routinely compelled to choose either a liberal arts and sciences pathway or a professional pathway just to fill out their college applications."

FIGURE 6

A FRAGMENTED CURRICULUM: MANY COURSES, FEW CONNECTIONS

Core Subjects in the Schools

The National Commission on Excellence in Education (1983) made influential recommendations for the four years of high school. Most states are still working to meet these goals for all students.

4 years	English
3 years	Social studies
3 years	Science
3 years	Mathematics
½ year	Computer science
2 years	Foreign language (for college-bound students)

Statewide Guidelines for General Education Distribution Requirements at the College Level

Forty states provide guidelines for general education for all public institutions in the state, for a system within the state, and/or to guide student transfer. Almost all conform to the following general pattern:

1–2 courses	Writing
3–4 courses	Arts and Humanities
2–3 courses	Social Sciences
2 courses	Science
1 course	Mathematics

Five states have made global and/or intercultural studies a requirement, and several others specify particular disciplines.

Sources: The National Commission on Excellence in Education, *A Nation at Risk: The Imperative for Educational Reform: A Report to the Nation and the Secretary of Education* (Washington, DC: U.S. Department of Education, 1983); Robert Shoenberg, ed., *General Education and Student Transfer: Fostering Intentionality and Coherence in State Systems* (Washington, DC: Association of American Colleges and Universities, 2005).

The expected curriculum is usually defined, often with enabling state regulation, in terms of specific "core" subjects in school and specific general education categories in college (see fig. 6). State "distribution" requirements for students' general education courses are the far-reaching legacy of the mid-twentieth-century view that equated liberal education with general education, and assigned it to the first two years of college.

But the frontiers of knowledge, both in scholarship and the world of work, now call for cross-disciplinary inquiry, analysis, and application. The major issues and problems of our time—from ensuring global sustainability to negotiating international markets to expanding human freedom—transcend individual disciplines. The core subjects provide a necessary foundation, but they should not be taught as ends in themselves. From school through college, students also need rich opportunities to explore "big questions" through multifaceted perspectives drawn from multiple disciplines.

Even in terms of the old modular curriculum, where each subject has been implicitly defined as a self-contained area of learning, the curricular pathways from school to college have become chaotic and redundant. Thanks to the vigorous promotion of Advanced Placement courses and dual enrollment (college courses for high school students), as many as three million students are already taking "college-level" courses before finishing the twelfth grade.[28] At the same time, because of the shortcomings of school preparation, at least 40 percent of all college students have to take at least one remedial course in college, essentially revisiting material that they should have learned in high school.[29]

Calls for aligning high school outcomes with college-level skills abound. But the learning students need for this new global era cannot be achieved simply by rearranging the existing patchwork of "core courses" at the school level and "general education requirements" at the college level. To help students achieve the essential learning outcomes, it will be necessary to spend time, across all levels of school and college education, revisiting the larger purposes of education and rethinking the kinds of connections across disciplines and levels of learning that will best prepare graduates for a complex and fast-paced world.

Key Questions to Guide School–College Planning

The following questions, keyed to twenty-first-century challenges, are intended to spark the needed school–college dialogues—among educators, across disciplines, with employers and policy leaders, and with the wider public. Ultimately, these questions call for the mapping of more purposeful curricular pathways, from school through college and across the disciplines.

How can we ensure that graduates are well prepared to participate in an interdependent global community?

"The Global Situation: The benefits of development are not shared equitably…. Injustice, poverty, ignorance, and violent conflict are widespread and the cause of great suffering…. The foundations of global security are threatened. These trends are perilous—but not inevitable."

—*The Earth Charter*

Global integration is now our shared context. The potential benefits of global interdependence are extraordinary, but so too are the challenges. Wealth, income, and social power are dramatically unequal within and across international boundaries. We are reminded daily of the clash of cultures, histories, and worldviews. The globe itself is fragile and vulnerable as are our shared civic spaces. These global challenges will be with us for the foreseeable future. Yet today, less than 10 percent of four-year graduates are leaving college globally prepared.[30] The United States is a world power. But it provides most of its students with a parochial education.

In this new era of interdependence, how should Americans prepare to contribute to a shared and sustainable future? What should Americans learn about the global economy and its changing dynamics? About world ecosystems and our capacity to sustain them? About the United States as a world power? About the realms of human heritage, cultures, religions, and laws, as well as the continuing quests to advance human dignity and justice? And, in this era of fundamentalisms and competing certainties, how will students engage and learn with people whose worldviews, histories, beliefs, and aspirations may be different in crucial ways from their own?

How can we prepare graduates for a global economy in which change and innovation are constants?

"The way forward is to become more open, more experimental, and to embrace the unknown….The bar for innovation is rising. And simply running in place will not be enough."

—The Council on Competitiveness

Innovation is widely touted as America's most important competitive advantage and the key to continued prosperity. But the currently dominant educational practices in American education were forged over a century ago, in an era that placed high value on broad understanding, reasoning, and abstract analysis and that gave only passing educational attention to collaboration, problem solving with external communities, and learning from experience.

In the context of a global economy that demands innovation, technological savvy, entrepreneurship, and risk taking, what kinds of educational practices will prepare graduates to get things done in the world? How do we teach them to critically evaluate the quality of information and convert this information into knowledge and action? How will students learn to solve problems effectively in collaboration with people from very different backgrounds and cultures? How will we teach students to combine entrepreneurial creativity and technological know-how with humanistic values and vision?

How can we prepare all graduates for a world shaped by scientific and technological advances and challenges?

"Together, we must ensure that U.S. students and workers have the grounding in math and science that they need to succeed and that mathematicians, scientists and engineers do not become an endangered species in the United States."

—The Business Roundtable

"The United States is a world power. But it provides most of its students with a parochial education."

Americans have grown accustomed to world leadership in science, technology, engineering, and mathematics (the STEM fields). As a society, we take for granted the unprecedented prosperity that this world leadership provides. But the majority of Americans are scientifically illiterate.[31]

What progression of studies, beginning in school and continuing in college, will dramatically raise the level of STEM preparation and literacy for all students? How do we reverse the alarming trends that show Americans falling steadily behind *both* in the percentage of college graduates who prepare in STEM fields *and* in the actual numbers of Americans who go on to successful careers in science and technology?[32] How can we persuade all Americans that STEM literacies are essential rather than a special option reserved for the gifted? What will be required to dramatically change the way STEM fields are taught so that the majority of Americans will no longer be left behind?

What kinds of learning are needed for knowledgeable and responsible citizenship?

"The death of democracy is not likely to be an assassination from ambush. It will be a slow extinction from apathy, indifference, and undernourishment."
—*Robert Maynard Hutchins*

Americans live in the world's most powerful democracy. But democracy, as the founders recognized, is much more than a design for government and lawmaking. Rather, it is a framework for a special kind of society in which citizens must take mutual responsibility for the quality of their own communities and their shared lives. Democracies are founded on a distinctive web of values: human dignity, equality, justice, responsibility, and freedom. The meanings and applications of these values are rarely self-evident and frequently contested. Moreover, most students never actually study such issues in any formal way, either in school or in college. Many students, the research shows, do not think that civic engagement is even a goal for their college studies.[33]

What are the complementary roles of school and postsecondary education in educating citizens? What is the particular role of college in preparing graduates to contribute to the greater good, both at home and abroad? What should Americans learn about the history and prospects for democracy, in our own society and in other parts of the world? How do we cultivate what Martha Nussbaum has called the "narrative imagination" so that graduates are better able to engage diverse communities and other societies?[34] How do we prepare citizens to address the growing and destabilizing divisions between those with hope and those who still live on the margins of our own and other societies?

How do we help graduates compose lives of meaning and integrity?

"It is difficult / to get the news from poems / yet men die miserably every day / for lack / of what is found there"
—*William Carlos Williams*

Throughout history, liberal education—and especially the arts and humanities—have been a constant resource, not just for civic life but for the inner life of self-discovery, values, moral inspiration,

"Democracies are founded on a distinctive web of values: human dignity, equality, justice, responsibility, and freedom. Most students never actually study such issues in any formal way, either in school or in college."

spiritual quests and solace, and the deep pleasures of encountering beauty, insight, and expressive power. Ultimately, it is this dimension—serious engagement with questions of values, principles, and larger meanings—that marks the essential difference between instrumental learning and liberal learning. For communities and individuals that are denied social power and voice, the arts and humanities make possible what Azar Nafisi calls "the Republic of the Imagination," a space where those who have been marginalized and persecuted can draw courage and hope from stories, language, culture, and example.[35] For all human beings, the arts and humanities invite exploration of the big and enduring questions about what it means to be human. They also foster the crucial human and civic capacity of empathy, the ability to care about and even identify with perspectives and circumstances other than one's own. The moral power of the arts and humanities has been one of the secrets of their lasting influence; those who experience these sources of inspiration readily see their importance, both for the human spirit and for community.

In this new century, the dizzying pace of change and the unabated prospects for social and environmental disruption will continue to place enormous strains on individuals as well as communities. Each individual will need sources of inner fortitude, self-knowledge, and personal renewal. Taking time for reflection on one's own values will be crucial. Everyone will need to consider not just how to pursue a course of action, but the value and integrity of alternative courses of action.

How, in this kind of environment, do we prepare students to cultivate their own inner resources of spirit and moral courage? How do we enable them to engage moral and social dilemmas with clarity about their own values as well as the capacity to hear and respond to others' deeply held commitments? How do we prepare graduates to make difficult ethical choices in the face of competing pressures? And how, without proselytizing, do we foster students' own development of character, conscience, and examined values?

Fulfilling the Promise of College in the Twenty-first Century

In college and university classrooms, in think tanks, in business organizations, and in government and corporate offices across the country, thoughtful people have begun to discuss the key questions with a new sense of urgency. Commissions have formed; reports are starting to multiply; resolve is growing. And, on many college campuses, one can find substantial centers of innovation where dedicated groups of faculty and staff already are responding creatively to just these kinds of questions. Many have invented impressive interdisciplinary curricula that engage learners brilliantly with every one of the questions outlined above. There are dozens of active reform movements across every facet of collegiate learning—from the first to the final year, and between the curriculum and student life.

To date, however, both these emerging discussions and the educational changes inspired by them are too preliminary, too fragmented,

---

LIBERAL EDUCATION AND VALUES

"Liberally educated students are curious about new intellectual questions, open to alternative ways of viewing a situation or problem, disciplined to follow intellectual methods to conclusions, capable of accepting criticism from others, tolerant of ambiguity, and respectful of others with different views. They understand and accept the imperative of academic honesty. Personal development is a very real part of intellectual development."

—AAC&U Board of Directors' Statement on Academic Freedom and Educational Responsibility

> *"The most significant reforms advance without reference to one another, and there is no shared sense of the whole."*

and far too limited. New approaches are emerging. (For a list of effective educational practices, see appendix A.) But these are too often relegated to the margins of institutional life. Many of the most significant reforms advance without reference to one another, and there is no shared sense of the whole. As a result, the impact on student learning is fragmented and diluted.

These discussions do not yet include the public, nor have they had much impact on education policy at the state and national levels. In fact, for the public universities and community colleges that educate over 75 percent of college students,[36] state requirements concerning "general education" are locked into an old system of required credits in specific areas of study (a few courses each in the arts and humanities, social sciences, and sciences) that functions today as a resistant barrier to the innovative curricula many faculty members want to create (see fig. 6 on p. 20).

The twentieth-century legacy of relegating liberal/general education to the first two years of college alone was codified across the nation. But that code has become a stranglehold on educational creativity and needs revision.

Students, for the most part, have been left entirely out of the debates about their own long-term educational interests. It is the nation's first-generation and less advantaged students—young and old alike—who are the most likely to enroll in institutions and programs that provide narrow training. First-generation students also are less likely than others to take courses in mathematics, science, social studies, humanities, history, foreign languages, or even computer science.[37] First-generation students are flocking to college. But many are missing out on a twenty-first-century education.

Because the prospects for American society are dependent on the quality of learning, insider discussions and educational reforms that mainly serve the most fortunate are inadequate. It is time to create a genuinely inclusive national dialogue about higher learning in the twenty-first century, and to embrace a vision for the future that is worthy of a great democracy.

And it is time to mobilize new determination and new leadership commitments—on the part of educators, policy makers, and the public as a whole—to advance substantially our national investment in educationally effective practices that can help all students understand, prepare for, and achieve the important outcomes of a twenty-first-century liberal education.

PART 3

A New Framework for Excellence

★ ★ ★ ★ ★ ★ ★ ★ ★ ★ ★ ★ ★ ★ ★ ★

The aims and outcomes described as "essential" in part 1 of this report (see p. 12) call for students to become "intentional learners" who focus, across ascending levels of study, on achieving these learning outcomes. But to help students do this, educational communities will also have to become more intentional both about these essential outcomes and about effective educational practices that help students integrate their learning and apply it to complex questions.

The principles and recommendations presented here are intended to give impetus to this new intentionality about the aims and quality of college learning, and about the complementary roles of school and college in preparing graduates for twenty-first-century realities.

In shaping the principles, the National Leadership Council for Liberal Education and America's Promise has drawn from many sources: active reform movements on many campuses and in a broad array of disciplines; recommendations from academic leaders; analyses from the business community; new standards in the accrediting communities; and dialogues held across the United States with campus, business, and community leaders.

The council believes that higher education can and should play a crucial role in fulfilling America's promise in this new global century: tapping potential, creating opportunity, fueling an innovative economy, reducing inequities, solving problems, and inspiring citizens to create a more just, humane, and sustainable world.

Toward these ends, the LEAP National Leadership Council calls for a new compact—between educators and American society—to adopt and enact the following seven Principles of Excellence.

"This new era calls on higher education to set significantly higher standards for student achievement while avoiding the disadvantages of standardization."

The Principles of Excellence

★ ★ ★ ★ ★ ★ ★ ★ ★ ★ ★ ★ ★ ★ ★ ★

Principle One

★ Aim High—and Make Excellence Inclusive

Make the Essential Learning Outcomes a Framework for the Entire Educational Experience, Connecting School, College, Work, and Life

Principle Two

★ Give Students a Compass

Focus Each Student's Plan of Study on Achieving the Essential Learning Outcomes— and Assess Progress

Principle Three

★ Teach the Arts of Inquiry and Innovation

Immerse All Students in Analysis, Discovery, Problem Solving, and Communication, Beginning in School and Advancing in College

Principle Four

★ Engage the Big Questions

Teach through the Curriculum to Far-Reaching Issues—Contemporary and Enduring— in Science and Society, Cultures and Values, Global Interdependence, the Changing Economy, and Human Dignity and Freedom

Principle Five

★ Connect Knowledge with Choices and Action

Prepare Students for Citizenship and Work through Engaged and Guided Learning on "Real-World" Problems

Principle Six

★ Foster Civic, Intercultural, and Ethical Learning

Emphasize Personal and Social Responsibility, in Every Field of Study

Principle Seven

★ Assess Students' Ability to Apply Learning to Complex Problems

Use Assessment to Deepen Learning and to Establish a Culture of Shared Purpose and Continuous Improvement

LEAP

★ Principle One
Aim High—and Make Excellence Inclusive

Make the Essential Learning Outcomes a Framework for the Entire Educational Experience, Connecting School, College, Work, and Life

Americans have entered a global century that presents "greater expectations" for knowledge in every area of life. This new era calls on higher education to set significantly higher standards for student achievement while avoiding the disadvantages of standardization. The essential learning outcomes (see p. 12) provide a common framework and a shared sense of direction for student accomplishment across school and college. These outcomes are not intended as a checklist of courses and requirements to—in the current campus vernacular—"get out of the way." Nor do they dictate a particular set of courses that all students should take.

Rather, these aims and outcomes are intended to build students' working understanding of the world and to foster capacities that will be practiced in school and used beyond school. The essential learning outcomes provide an inclusive framework for a contemporary liberal education by defining it not as a selected set of disciplines, but as a set of resources for all aspects of life: work, citizenship, and personal fulfillment.

Contemporary students compose their education across many different institutions and from many different academic fields and courses. Of those who complete a bachelor's degree, nearly 60 percent take courses at more than one college or university and nearly 25 percent at more than two institutions.[38] The essential learning outcomes set a common framework that provides a sense of purpose and direction to guide student progress across the many different parts of the academic system. The outcomes can be used for P–16 planning in the states, articulation between two-year and four-year colleges and universities, and accreditation standards for institutions and academic fields. At every level, a clear and constant focus on these essential outcomes can help systems, institutions, academic programs, and students themselves become more intentional.

These forms of learning can and should be fostered through many different curricular pathways. But to ensure their achievement, each institution and each program will need to be certain that students have multiple opportunities and appropriate academic support to work toward the intended outcomes. To reach high levels of success, each system, each institution, and each academic program will need to set standards and guidelines for the expected level of student accomplishment.

Within higher education, many will see these aims and outcomes as goals for the general education program alone. *That is not the intention.* General education plays a role in their fulfillment. But it is not feasible to assign to general education programs alone the breadth and scope of learning described in the essential learning outcomes. The majors also have a crucial role to play in fostering rich knowledge, strong intellectual and practical skills, an examined sense of personal

---

THE PRINCIPLES IN PRACTICE
Aim High—and Make Excellence Inclusive

The State Council of Higher Education for Virginia (SCHEV) has identified a set of competencies that all students should achieve from their college studies. The competencies are similar to the "intellectual and practical skills" that the LEAP National Leadership Council defines as "essential." SCHEV requires public institutions to submit "reports of institutional effectiveness" that include assessments of student learning in written communication, technology/information literacy, quantitative reasoning, scientific reasoning, critical thinking, and oral communication. Each individual campus defines the outcomes, establishes expected achievement levels, creates or chooses assessment methods, and reports on results. The SCHEV framework creates public and transparent reports of institutional learning outcomes while maintaining institutional autonomy to define and assess student learning outcomes in relation to institutional mission and priorities.

THE PRINCIPLES IN PRACTICE
Aim High—and Make Excellence Inclusive

Faculty at **Indiana University–Purdue University Indianapolis** (IUPUI) have agreed to six Principles of Undergraduate Learning that define important learning outcomes for each IUPUI student. These include communication and quantitative skills; critical thinking; intellectual depth, breadth, and adaptiveness; integration and application of knowledge; understanding society and culture; and values and ethics. These principles apply to the entire educational experience and to the departmental programs as well as general education courses. Most students take a first-year learning community that explores these core goals and helps students begin work on them. To document and assess students' achievement, IUPUI faculty are developing e-portfolios that set standards for the outcomes and make the basis for their assessments visible. IUPUI has provided extensive support for faculty development as well as student orientation as it encourages this shift toward goals across the entire educational experience.

and social responsibility, and the ability to integrate and apply knowledge from many different contexts. If the majors neglect these shared goals, students are unlikely to achieve them.

Recommendation 1

The National Leadership Council recommends that a national commitment be made to foster the aims and outcomes of a twenty-first-century liberal education for all college students, not just those attending elite institutions and not just those studying in what traditionally have been called "arts and sciences disciplines."

This call is extended to each college, community college, and university; to state systems; and to the fields of study within colleges and universities. Every institution and system should develop for itself a vision of intended learning outcomes that addresses, in ways appropriate to mission, the multiple goals for college. This vision should be expressed in a public document that is accessible to everyone and frequently consulted by faculty, staff, and students alike. In state systems, the educational outcomes should become shared responsibilities, applicable across institutional boundaries.

Every field should be taught as part of liberal education, and every field should audit, clarify, and strengthen its own practices for fostering the knowledge and capacities identified as essential outcomes of a twenty-first-century education.

Recommendation 2

The National Leadership Council recommends that two-year colleges, together with the senior institutions that serve large numbers of transfer students, focus on the aims and outcomes of a twenty-first-century liberal education.

Nearly half the nation's college students, and the majority of students from low-income families, begin their studies in two-year institutions.[39] It should be a national priority to ensure that these students, whatever their career choices and preparation, become richly prepared for a changing economy, for the option of further study, and for a lifetime of continuous learning—as employees and as citizens.

This recommendation neither requires nor anticipates that community college students should study only, or primarily, what are conventionally known as arts and sciences or "general education" courses. Rather, it calls on two-year and four-year institutions, in every state and region, to collaboratively remap the curriculum so that arts and sciences and professional or "career" courses can work together, from first to final years, to foster the broad knowledge, sophisticated skills, personal and social responsibility, and demonstrated achievement that every student needs and deserves.

Faculty and staff who teach remedial/developmental courses should take an active part in this remapping, so that these courses help students prepare successfully for the expectations and standards of the regular curriculum.

★ Principle Two
Give Students a Compass

Focus Each Student's Plan of Study on Achieving the Essential Learning Outcomes—and Assess Progress

American college students already know that they want a degree. The challenge is to help students become highly intentional about the forms of learning and accomplishment that the degree should represent

In today's academy, many students are not following any comprehensive academic plan at all. Rather, many are working to cobble together a sufficient number of courses that will enable them to meet the required number of credits—typically 60 at the associate's level and 120 at the bachelor's level—necessary to earn a degree. Setting goals for educational accomplishment based on the essential learning outcomes can change this haphazard approach to academic study. Each student will know what is expected, and each student can construct a plan of study that simultaneously addresses his or her own interests and assures achievement in the essential learning outcomes.

Students will know before they enter college, for example, that they are expected to bring their communication skills—written and oral—to a high level of demonstrated accomplishment. As they work with mentors to plan a course of study, they will learn to seek out, rather than avoid, courses in which extensive writing and/or oral presentations are required. The same principle applies to all the outcomes. By clarifying the intended forms of learning and their significance, and by helping students connect these broad outcomes with their own individual goals and areas of study, educators will help all students become more intentional about their learning and more likely to reach high levels of accomplishment.

Recommendation 3

The National Leadership Council recommends that the essential learning outcomes be used to guide each student's plan of study and cumulative learning and, further, that their achievement be the shared focus of both school and college.

Students should begin intensive work in each of these areas of learning—knowledge, skills, responsibilities, and integrative learning—as early as middle school. And they should understand that they will be expected—wherever they enroll, whatever their intended career, and no matter how far they go in college—to attain progressively higher levels of competence in each of these key areas. Teachers, faculty members, and student life professionals should work together to help students understand why these outcomes are important, and how they are applied in work settings, civil society, and students' own lives.

"Setting goals for educational accomplishment based on the essential learning outcomes can change this haphazard approach to academic study."

THE PRINCIPLES IN PRACTICE

Give Students a Compass

The curriculum at **Bard College** is designed to encourage students to play an active and intentional role in shaping their education. Rather than selecting from traditional departmental majors, students at Bard major in programs that cross disciplinary boundaries. This program-based approach is combined with core curricular experiences that develop broad capacities and allow for milestone assessments of learning. New students begin their studies with the Workshop in Language and Thinking, an intensive summer program that serves as an introduction to college-level learning, and continue in the first-year seminar, where they explore many of the intellectual ideas that will form the basis of their subsequent study. In the second semester of the sophomore year, students undertake "moderation," a process that requires them to reflect on their academic experiences, assess their performance, and plan in consultation with faculty advisers the work they will pursue in their major field. This culminates with the senior project, which serves as the capstone to a Bard education. Together, these elements of the college's curriculum help students to integrate their learning and follow a purposeful course of study as they chart a path through their undergraduate education.

Recommendation 4

The National Leadership Council recommends that teachers and faculty set high and explicit standards for student achievement, that the curriculum be organized to provide students with ample opportunities to meet the standards, and that students be provided with regular feedback on their progress.

The expected standards should be made public, and should periodically be reviewed by external experts to ensure appropriate quality. While in high school, students should receive periodic feedback about their progress, as well as guidance on the connections between the expected outcomes and future success in both work and college. Diagnostic assessments in the first year of college, and milestone assessments upon completion of community college and/or the second year of college, can help students evaluate their own achievement to date and identify areas of needed improvement. Each student's plan of study—informed by the assessments—should clearly connect expected outcomes to the institution's required studies, students' major field(s), and their elective choices. Where today's students frequently see curricular requirements as a set of obstacles to get "behind them" as early as possible, the students of tomorrow will know that learning is cumulative and that continuous progress is both expected and supported.

★ **Principle Three**

Teach the Arts of Inquiry and Innovation

Immerse All Students in Analysis, Discovery, Problem Solving, and Communication, Beginning in School and Advancing in College

In a complex world, there is no way that students can master everything they "need to know." The scope is too broad, and the frontiers of knowledge are expanding far too rapidly. The key to educational excellence, therefore, lies not in the memorization of vast amounts of information, but rather in fostering habits of mind that enable students to continue their learning, engage new questions, and reach informed judgments. Helping students master analytical capacities has been one of the most enduring commitments of a liberal education. Since this nation was founded, American leaders have emphasized the value of these capacities to a free society; today, we see their value for an innovation-fueled economy as well.

Given their importance, the foundations for inquiry, investigation, and discovery should be laid early and reinforced across the educational system. A good education should provide multiple opportunities for students to engage in "inquiry-based learning," both independently and in collaborative teams. Through inquiry projects, students should learn how to find and evaluate evidence, how to consider and assess competing interpretations, how to form and test their own analyses and interpretations, how to solve problems, and how to communicate persuasively.

Fifty years ago, it would not have been feasible to emphasize inquiry and discovery in many fields and institutions. Today, however, the advent of new technologies has created unprecedented opportunities for students to take part in collaborative inquiry, creative projects, and research. The need and the opportunity are there. Yet most schools and colleges have barely tested the waters. Faculty members who supervise student research and/or teach "capstone" courses to advanced college students frequently are frustrated by students' poor preparation for tackling complex inquiry and creative projects. That is because few departments and institutions have developed curricula and pedagogies that incrementally foster and assess students' skills in inquiry and innovation as they advance through a course of study. Fundamental change is needed, at all levels of education, to help students develop the intellectual and practical skills basic to inquiry, innovation, and effective communication.

Recommendation 5

The National Leadership Council recommends that the power of new technologies be harnessed in order to give all students extensive experience in research, experimentation, problem-based learning, and other forms of creative work, especially but not only in their major fields.

Undergraduates today, even first-year students, can learn how to use tools of research, analysis, design, and creation that are more powerful than those available to professionals a generation ago. Whether the challenge is studying classical Greece, designing semiconductors, analyzing elections, or extending access to the arts, the technological tools available to students are extraordinary. The Internet and other communications technologies also make it possible for students to take part in creative problem solving with partners outside of the classroom—community agencies, arts organizations, corporations, schools, and people in other parts of the world. Technology-assisted inquiry should be carefully woven into the expected academic experience and emphasized in the college majors.

Recommendation 6

The National Leadership Council recommends that colleges and universities work with the schools to raise the level of inquiry and project-based learning in precollegiate education and take vigorous steps to build these skills further once students enter college.

The best public and private schools and many of the most successful charter schools have long made analysis and inquiry central to their programs of high school preparation and learning. But in many schools, students write very little and receive no preparation in critical inquiry and research skills. When this foundation is lacking, colleges must play catch-up when it should be their primary task to move students' skills in analysis and application to a much higher level. New emphasis on the skills essential to inquiry and innovation is needed

- in the preparation of teachers and faculty;
- in the design of curriculum and assessments in the schools;

THE PRINCIPLES IN PRACTICE
Teach the Arts of Inquiry and Innovation

With the support of a Ewing Marion Kauffman Foundation grant, the **University of Rochester** is striving to make entrepreneurship—and the skills that accompany it such as problem solving, continuous learning, and innovation—a basic component of undergraduate education by infusing it into all academic disciplines. The University of Rochester has created the Center for Entrepreneurship (CFE), which brings together faculty, students, and community members from a variety of academic disciplines to encourage and enhance the culture of entrepreneurship at the university and within the Rochester community. As a result, there are now courses at the University of Rochester available for students wishing to focus specifically on entrepreneurship as it relates to any major, and the CFE holds a variety of workshops, seminars, and conferences for faculty as well. The University of Rochester is one of several dozen liberal arts colleges and research universities that are connecting entrepreneurship with teaching, learning, and research in arts and sciences disciplines.

"The key to educational excellence lies not in the memorization of vast amounts of information, but rather in fostering habits of mind that enable students to continue their learning, engage new questions, and reach informed judgments."

THE PRINCIPLES IN PRACTICE

TEACH THE ARTS OF INQUIRY AND INNOVATION

Curricular strategy	Transparency	Classroom practices	Example
Step 1. In high school, students enroll in a theme-based academy of three or four linked courses that promote synthesis through projects.	Advisers and teachers stress the goals of answering questions and justifying the answers, framing new questions, and relating raw data to the questions.	Teachers provide guiding questions, prompts, models, frameworks, and suggested sites for information. They use direct observation, case studies, simulations, and role playing.	**Sir Francis Drake High School (San Anselmo, California)** Students study the election process by creating video campaign ads for candidates or issues in an upcoming election. They also make "process" Web sites that lead them to reflect upon their learning and thinking.
Step 2. In college, first-year seminars and selected courses in general education introduce inquiry and analysis through specific problems/projects/assignments.	Professors make explicit the outcomes of further developing powers of observation, synthesis, and problem posing as well as expectations in reflection and analysis. Critical thinking is stressed as a goal of the first-year seminars/courses and of the entire institution.	Writing assignments and/or oral presentations ask students to identify a problem/issue and devise ways to resolve it. Professors provide guidelines and format. Techniques might include journals, brainstorming, teamwork, or demonstrations.	**Indiana University–Purdue University Indianapolis** A first-year learning community for students in engineering includes an investigation of reverse engineering, instruction on creating a Web page, an introduction to engineering careers, and a look at professional organizations. It also includes a group research paper, teamwork topics, and a PowerPoint presentation.
Step 3. Across the college curriculum, problem-based learning occurs in disciplinary courses as students begin their majors.	Professors discuss critical observation, problem posing and problem solving, analysis, synthesis, and interpretation of complex issues in the discipline. At the institutional level, facilities support problem-based learning and inquiry is stressed as an institutional priority for all majors.	Projects based on complex issues/problems of the field ask students to draw on their specific content knowledge as well as on their developing powers of analysis, synthesis, and interpretation. Students pose their own questions and devise ways of answering them. Active, hands-on learning could alternate with lectures that provide "just-in-time" information that students can apply immediately.	**Samford University (Birmingham, Alabama)** A junior-year, foundational nursing course includes a problem-based learning model for each key concept. Progressing through the course involves advancing from simple to complex concepts. A module, which might last from several days to one month, could focus, for example, on nutrition and hygiene issues in nursing patients from diverse cultural and religious traditions. Students form groups early in the course to work through the problems posed.
Step 4. At the senior level, a capstone project or thesis in the major (or in general education) culminates the inquiry approach to learning by asking students to draw on the knowledge and skills acquired in the major, general education, electives, and cocurricular experiences.	Course catalogs and departmental information about the senior capstone experience clearly state that the capstone requires advanced critical analysis, evidence, synthesis, conceptualization, interpretation, and evaluation. Formative assessments during the experience provide reminders of the need for insightful use of data, logic, and diverse resources.	Under faculty guidance, students or teams choose a significant problem/project to research/carry out over a semester or two. The professor could provide guiding questions but the emphasis is on student initiative. The work could be made public through publishing an article or presenting it to community and industry experts.	**Southern Illinois University Edwardsville** All seniors must complete a capstone that, for computer science majors, consists of a team project that spans two semesters. Ideas for real programming needs are solicited from the university and local community. Students are responsible for all aspects, from establishing initial requirements to implementation and deployment; they need to figure out how to interact with and design products for non-specialist users.

Adapted from Andrea Leskes and Ross Miller, *Purposeful Pathways: Helping Students Achieve Key Learning Outcomes* (Washington, DC: Association of American Colleges and Universities, 2006), 37.

- as students progress from year to year;
- in the college admissions process, which ought to attend more closely to student experience in inquiry- and project-based learning;
- in the careful design of first-year and second-year experiences geared to students' differing levels of preparation and skill;
- in the careful design of advanced studies that emphasize inquiry, analysis, and the application of knowledge to complex problems.

In recalibrating school and college curricula, and the connections between them, educators need to ensure that every student experiences the excitement and intellectual growth that follows from working to solve real problems. In doing so, they will also provide students with the forms of preparation they need both for a dynamic and innovative economy and for a vibrant democracy.

★ **Principle Four**

Engage the Big Questions

Teach through the Curriculum to Far-Reaching Issues—Contemporary and Enduring—in Science and Society, Cultures and Values, Global Interdependence, the Changing Economy, and Human Dignity and Freedom

Study in the arts and sciences remains an essential and integral part of a twenty-first-century liberal education. But it is time to challenge the idea—tacitly but solidly established in American education—that simply taking a prescribed number of courses in liberal arts and sciences fields is sufficient. Rather, new steps must be taken to ensure that study in these core disciplines prepares students to engage with the "big questions," both contemporary and enduring. Study in the arts and sciences should provide students with opportunities to explore the enduring issues, questions, and problems they confront as human beings—questions of meaning, purpose, and moral integrity. These studies should also teach students to look beyond themselves, by considering their obligations to others, and to look beyond the classroom, by applying their analytical skills and learning to significant issues and problems in the world around them.

The research on this point is compelling. All students—including those least prepared—learn best when they can see the point of what they are doing. Illuminating real-world implications can help students discover the excitement and the benefits of powerful learning.[40]

By engaging students with complex issues, questions, and problems where there are real consequences at stake, and by teaching students how to draw and assess knowledge from many sources, this problem-centered approach to liberal education will prepare students both for the challenges of a dynamic global economy and for the responsibilities of citizenship.

To achieve this vision, it will be necessary to revisit the chaotic and redundant practices that currently subvert powerful learning in both school and college. Millions of college students are presently repeat-

---

THE PRINCIPLES IN PRACTICE

Engage the Big Questions

In addition to core general education requirements, **San Jose State University** (SJSU) has implemented SJSU Studies, which are intended to foster students' advanced, integrative learning as citizens and thoughtful people. Each SJSU undergraduate must take one upper-level class in each of four topic areas—Earth and Environment; Self, Society, and Equality in the United States; Culture, Civilization, and Global Understanding; and Written Communication. These courses connect the curriculum to larger, complex issues in society as a way of preparing students to become better global citizens and educated adults. Like many campuses in the California State University system, San Jose State University serves many transfer students who have taken all or many of their core general education requirements at other institutions. By framing distinctive upper-level goals for general education, SJSU affirms its commitment—officially endorsed by the Faculty Senate—to liberal education for all students. It also creates its own "signature" approach to that goal.

"It is time to challenge the idea that simply taking a prescribed number of courses in liberal arts and sciences fields is sufficient."

"Illuminating real-world implications can help students discover the excitement and the benefits of powerful learning."

THE PRINCIPLES IN PRACTICE

Engage the Big Questions

One of seven colleges in the Dallas County Community College system, **Richland College** serves nearly twenty thousand students who collectively speak seventy-nine different first languages. Richland's several academic enrichment programs reinforce the college's emphasis on educating students to build sustainable communities, both at home and abroad. The Global Studies program, for example, challenges students to search for solutions to issues such as "peace, ecological balance, social and economic justice, intercultural understanding, democratic participation, and the impact of technology." By design, Global Studies intersects with other academic enrichment programs, including Richland's campuswide service-learning program, learning communities (two courses that address a common topic from different disciplinary perspectives), peace studies, and several ethnic studies programs. To earn a Global Studies Certificate—which complements other majors—students take fifteen hours of Global Studies courses, including a learning community, and also complete an academically based service-learning project. Students who take one year of a second language and earn honors grades are named Global Studies Scholars. With a strong emphasis on integrative planning and continuous educational improvement, Richland College became in 2006 the first community college to win the Malcolm Baldrige National Quality Award, the nation's highest presidential recognition for quality and organizational excellence.

ing work they should have accomplished in high school, and paying college tuition to do so. At the same time, three million students are now taking "early college courses" that give them a leg up on college-level requirements, especially in arts and sciences fields.[41] Often, however, students can use these early college credits to avoid further learning in core disciplines—such as science, mathematics, history, or languages—once they are enrolled in college. With the demand for advanced knowledge expanding exponentially, it is self-defeating to let today's college students opt out of key disciplines before they even begin their higher education. It is equally self-defeating to cover essentially the same content in both high school and college survey courses.

Therefore, a coordinated effort is needed to ensure that all Americans reach high levels of knowledge and skill—begun in school and advanced in college—in the following areas of twenty-first-century learning:

- **science, mathematics, and technology**—including a solid grasp of the methods by which scientific knowledge is tested, validated, and revised
- **cultural and humanistic literacy**—including knowledge of the world's histories, American history, philosophical traditions, major religions, diverse cultural legacies, and contested questions
- **global knowledge and competence**—including an understanding of economic forces, other cultures, interdependence, and political dynamics, as well as second-language competence and direct experience with cultural traditions other than one's own
- **civic knowledge and engagement**—including a rich understanding of the values and struggles that have established democratic institutions and expanded human freedom and justice, and direct experience in addressing the needs of the larger community
- **inquiry- and project-based learning**—including multiple opportunities to work, independently and collaboratively, on projects that require the integration of knowledge with skills in analysis, discovery, problem solving, and communication

This is not a menu of course categories. Rather, it is a proposal to move beyond the fragmented modular curriculum that students already take in the arts and sciences, in both school and college (see p. 20, fig. 6). **The list above specifies core areas of twenty-first-century learning** and invites fresh consideration of the way study within and across different disciplines—from school through college—can be organized to develop deep knowledge and strong competence in each of them.

Self-evidently, four years of study is not enough time to achieve such breadth and depth of knowledge. But students are spending at least sixteen years—if they complete a bachelor's degree—in the combination of school and college. If educators map goals for learning in these core areas across this extended sequence of study, the goals become attainable.

Recommendation 7

The National Leadership Council recommends that faculty and teachers in all the relevant disciplines be involved in new national efforts to identify the goals for college-level achievement in each of these core areas of twenty-first-century learning, and to create purposeful curricular pathways, from high school through college, that ensure students' cumulative learning in these core areas.

The task goes well beyond identifying needed knowledge in such basic disciplines as literature, history, or biology. Rather, educators should revisit the overarching goals for student learning in the arts and sciences, and create disciplinary and cross-disciplinary patterns of learning that build deep understanding of the world in which students live and work. Because these broad areas of learning illuminate the context for students' specialized interests, the core areas should be addressed across the several years of college, and not just in the first two years.

Recommendation 8

The National Leadership Council recommends that new efforts be made to raise the level of student engagement and accomplishment in these core areas of learning in both the final years of high school and the initial phase of college.

The transition from school to college should be the joint responsibility of schools and higher education, and should be carefully planned to ensure that students meet high standards in each of the core areas of expected learning. Standards should be set for needed levels of achievement in these essential areas of learning at the point of college entrance, and the final years of high school should be designed to ensure that students meet the expected entrance standards. Colleges should provide diagnostic feedback to their students on their actual level of preparation and achievement in these expected areas of twenty-first-century learning, and on what they need to accomplish further to meet the institution's own expectations for graduation-level knowledge and competence. At all points along the way, educators should work with external partners to help students understand why and how these core areas of learning are important to success in the economy and to the responsibilities of citizenship.

★ Principle Five
Connect Knowledge with Choices and Action

Prepare Students for Citizenship and Work through Engaged and Guided Learning on "Real-World" Problems

Both democracy and the economy depend on creative problem solving, bold experimentation, and the capacity to learn from the results of experimentation. As they move through their studies, students should have multiple opportunities to grapple with and prepare for these "real-world" demands. Assignments should compel them to define the task, explain its significance, test alternative

---

THE PRINCIPLES IN PRACTICE

Connect Knowledge with Choices and Action

The "practical liberal arts" are deeply embedded in **Wagner College**'s prize-winning college curriculum. The Wagner Plan requires students to complete issue-centered integrative learning communities (LCs) during the first year, the intermediate years, and the senior year. The LCs are organized around a big theme or problem and include experiential as well as academic learning. In the first year, students take two courses from different disciplines related to the overarching theme and complete an experiential field placement related to the LC theme in the New York metropolitan area. Students also complete a "reflective tutorial" which emphasizes writing and teaches them to evaluate and integrate their learning from different disciplines and from the field placement. A senior-year LC is linked to the student's major and acts as a capstone course, connecting knowledge from the major with practical applications in the student's chosen field. At graduation, Wagner students are already practiced in integrating knowledge learned inside and outside the classroom in the context of real-world problems and settings.

solutions, and take actions based on their own judgment. Some of these learning experiences can take the form of independent study; others should be carefully designed experiences in collaborative learning with diverse partners. Every student should prepare for both life and citizenship by working frequently on unscripted problems, and by building capacities to function as part of an effective team. Fostering this kind of informed practical judgment should be a priority for every academic field.

Students today have many opportunities for "learning in the field," including service-learning courses, internships, cooperative education, and community-based research. Some majors routinely include apprenticeship assignments, such as student teaching. Many students do projects with diverse communities and/or in other parts of the world as part of their formal study. And 90 percent of college students work while they are in school.[42]

While all these experiences present rich opportunities for connecting knowledge with choices and action, too many are essentially "add-ons" in which students are left to their own devices for any insights gained. Students perform service on their own time; they find jobs and even internships independently of their academic studies. Study abroad, another form of experiential learning, is powerful for students, but any educational "debriefing" on what they learned by living in another culture frequently goes on quite apart from their home institutions and departments. Work—especially off-campus employment—is too often considered a distraction rather than a potentially rich venue for applying what one is learning in the academic program.

To build students' preparation for both work and citizenship, higher education needs to give new emphasis to fostering practical judgment and problem solving "in the field." Community-based learning should be integrated into the curriculum, and efforts to strengthen the quality of students' learning from such experiences should become an integral part of a contemporary liberal education.

In fostering these kinds of practical judgment and problem solving, there is much to be learned from the professional fields and from the performing arts. As Lee Shulman and his colleagues at the Carnegie Foundation for the Advancement of Teaching have demonstrated, many of the signature practices of professional education are designed to help individuals develop their capacities for effective judgment in contexts where the right course of action is uncertain.[43] They do this by making the learner's thinking and assumptions public in the presence of knowledgeable mentors and peers and by subjecting these to intense discussion and challenge. Similarly, both in the professions and in the performing arts, the learner's performance itself is public, and students work closely with mentors on ways to improve the quality of their work. Learning to give and receive feedback is already part of both professional and artistic development; it ought to become expected practice in all fields of study.

To apply knowledge productively in field-based settings, all students should experience in-depth questioning from faculty, staff, and other mentors about their assumptions, analyses, conclusions, and actions. Learners also need both guidance and feedback, from mentors and peers, as they probe the facets of a complex issue and test their own insights against both theory and the experiences of others. And to prepare for the world's diversity, all students need frequent opportunities to engage in collaborative interaction with people whose assumptions and life experiences are different from their own.

Recommendation 9

The National Leadership Council recommends that every student engage in some form of field-based learning and that faculty and staff create opportunities (reflective forums) for students to learn collaboratively and systematically from their field-based experiences.

These opportunities can take many different forms to serve different educational fields and student learning goals. Models for good practice in experiential learning have already been developed in many professional and performing arts fields, in the service-learning community, and in some global studies programs. These models should be more widely studied and adopted. Each institution and program should review and strengthen its standards for supervising, supporting, and evaluating students' field-based learning.

Recommendation 10

The National Leadership Council recommends that partnerships between faculty and student life professionals be strengthened in order to integrate and document the learning students gain from involvement with a campus community.

Some of the most powerful learning in college occurs in activities undertaken as part of the cocurriculum, both on campus and through campus outreach to community partners. The essential learning outcomes can be fostered through intentional integration of students' in-class and out-of-class activities. There should be far more systematic attention paid to fostering these opportunities for guided experiential learning and to documenting, through expanded forms of assessment, the gains students make on the essential learning outcomes through these cocurricular experiences.

★ Principle Six
Foster Civic, Intercultural, and Ethical Learning
Emphasize Personal and Social Responsibility, in Every Field of Study

Since the founding of the United States, Americans have recognized the close connections between education and the sustainability of our democratic experiment. Traditionally, however, the role of producing an educated citizenry was assigned to the public schools, which enrolled almost everyone, rather than to higher education, which until recently served only a small fraction of the population.

THE PRINCIPLES IN PRACTICE

Foster Civic, Intercultural, and Ethical Learning

In 1994, **Portland State University** faculty adopted University Studies, a four-year general education program for all students. The program is organized around four broad goals: inquiry and critical thinking, communication, the diversity of human experience, and ethics and social responsibility. The culminating senior experience is a community-based learning course designed to provide interdisciplinary teams of students with the opportunity to apply what they have learned in their major and in their other University Studies courses to a real challenge emanating from the metropolitan community. These partnerships—designed to engage diverse communities for common purposes— are mutually beneficial ventures, as the organizations help students place their academic learning in a real-world context, and students assist organizations in meaningful projects such as grant writing, designing curriculum and educational materials, and serving as advocates for underserved populations and issues. Assessments show that the community work helps students become more aware of their own biases and prejudices and deepens students' understanding of sociopolitical issues. Students also develop a better understanding of how to make a difference in their own communities.

Reflecting this inherited division of labor, higher education is poised ambivalently between the past and the future concerning its appropriate role in fostering democratic values and responsibilities. Mission statements proclaim education for citizenship as central. They testify to the role of the academy in fostering personal and social responsibility, at home and abroad; in preparing graduates to contribute to the community; and more recently, in building communities that acknowledge and value difference.[44] But the faculty members who actually teach students rarely are asked to think deeply about their own responsibilities for educating engaged and ethical citizens. In practice, many assume that teaching students to think critically is the academy's main contribution to the public good.

During the last two decades, higher education has embarked on new efforts to foster civic engagement. A "service-learning movement" has gained strong traction on all kinds of campuses—large and small, two-year and four-year. Simultaneously, many faculty members have worked to make diversity studies and intercultural learning a new basic for student learning in college. Both service learning and experiences with diversity are powerful catalysts for deeper engagement and insight. They teach students to engage, respect, and learn from people with worldviews that are very different from their own. They involve students with many of society's most urgent unsolved problems. They challenge individuals to consider, at a deep level, the responsibilities of a democratic society to its citizens, and their own responsibilities as human beings and citizens. And these forms of learning have significant effects on students' ethical awareness, challenging learners to confront alternative beliefs and values, and to think more deeply about their own. Research studies show that service and diversity experiences have positive effects both on students' civic commitments and on their overall cognitive development.[45]

As with so many other "high-impact" educational innovations, these efforts to prepare students for active citizenship in diverse communities still hover on the margins of the mainstream academy. Some students participate and benefit; large numbers do not. Less than half of college seniors report that their college experience significantly influenced their capacity to contribute to their communities; only half report significant gains in learning about people from different backgrounds.[46] Moreover, there is searing evidence that study in many majors actually depresses students' interest in active citizenship.[47] This is a warning note indeed for a democracy that depends on civic responsibility and commitment.

The higher education community needs to match its commitment to educating responsible and ethical citizens with learning practices, in both the curriculum and cocurriculum, that help all college students engage their responsibilities to self and others. Further, vigorous efforts are needed to build new understanding that civic development—in all the forms described here—is an essential rather than an elective outcome of college.

Recommendation 11

The National Leadership Council recommends that students be provided with recurring opportunities to explore issues of civic, intercultural, and ethical responsibility in the context of their broad studies of science, cultures, and society and, further, that these topics be connected to democracy and global interdependence.

Questions about the relationship between individuals and societies, about major developments in human histories, and about cross-cultural encounters are classic themes for the shared curriculum, whether in a first-year experience, or a general education sequence, or in advanced capstone courses that provide a larger context for students' specialized studies. First-year and general education courses should intentionally help students grapple with the kinds of "big questions" they will inevitably face both as human beings and as citizens—about science and society, cultures and values, global interdependence, the changing economy, and human dignity and freedom. The general education curriculum is also a place where students can explore the values, institutions, and aspirations that are basic to democracy, examining these complex questions through multiple and cross-disciplinary lenses: philosophical, empirical, historical, cross-cultural.

The foundations for such studies need to be laid in the schools, through a course of study that builds rich understandings both of world histories and of American history, and of the relationships between them (see recommendation 7). Building on these precollegiate experiences, college courses can help students explore the difficult issues of our world, the ones where both the nature of the problem and the range of solutions are actively contested. Equally important, college forums can model and teach the kinds of respectful deliberation—across difficult differences—that are crucially important to a sustainable democracy.

Recommendation 12

The National Leadership Council recommends that students be provided with guided opportunities to explore civic, ethical, and intercultural issues in the context of their chosen fields.

Every field of study, no matter how "technical," is a community of practice. For this reason, no field is "value-free." Every community of practice is framed by communal values and ethical responsibilities; these expectations need to be made explicit and fully explored among students and faculty. Similarly, every field is rife with contested questions whose resolution may have far-reaching human consequences. In every community of practice, there are some people with power and others who lack and/or seek power. Often, questions of power are further complicated by legacies of racial, ethnic, gender, and other disparities. When students choose a field of study, they need and deserve the opportunity to explore openly all of the issues basic to their community with their fellow students and with guidance from mentors. They should have many occasions to clarify and apply their own sense of ethical, professional, and civic responsibilities as they move forward in their chosen course of study.

THE PRINCIPLES IN PRACTICE

Foster Civic, Intercultural, and Ethical Learning

Hundreds of colleges, community colleges, and universities now encourage students to take part in community service. But in the wake of Hurricane Katrina, **Tulane University** has taken service learning and civic engagement to another level. Tulane requires all students to make public service an integral part of their college studies, both in the core curriculum and in their advanced studies. To meet the public service graduation requirement, students must take one service-learning class during their first two years. During this time, students also create and maintain an e-portfolio that charts their progress and reflects on their service learning. In their later college years, students choose a second public service experience. This may be another service-learning course, a service-learning internship, a public service research project or honors thesis project, a service-based study abroad program, or a capstone experience that includes a public service component. The Center for Public Service sustains partnerships with community organizations that provide a context for students' public service commitments.

"The right standard for both assessment and accountability at the college level is students' demonstrated ability to apply their learning to complex, unscripted problems."

★ **Principle Seven**

Assess Students' Ability to Apply Learning to Complex Problems

Use Assessment to Deepen Learning and to Establish a Culture of Shared Purpose and Continuous Improvement

As affirmed throughout this report, the essential learning outcomes provide a shared framework for both intentionality and accountability, across the entire educational system, within the various sectors of higher education, and in students' own educational planning. Recommendation 4 calls on educators to create diagnostic, interim, and capstone assessments in order to give individual students feedback on their progress in achieving the expected outcomes in the context of their chosen course of study.

Especially in light of the high-stakes-testing movement in the schools, many will want to act immediately to identify standardized tests that can be used to establish how well students are doing on the recommended learning outcomes. The 2006 report from the federal Commission on the Future of Higher Education took this tack, recommending that every campus measure students' learning with standardized tests, and that the states aggregate and compare the results of various standardized measures.[48]

For two reasons, a rush to adopt standardized testing for higher education would prove to be a "low-yield" strategy.[49] First, the essential learning outcomes can be described in common, easily accessible language (see p. 12), but they are—in practice—complex capacities that are fostered and expressed quite differently in different fields. For example, both a teacher and a chemist will need skills in inquiry, information literacy, and writing, but their competence in applying these skills will be manifested in different ways. Thus, general tests of the recommended learning outcomes will not provide evidence about students' field-related achievement and competence. Field-specific tests, while available in many disciplines, do not generally assess students' mastery of higher-level intellectual, problem-solving, collaborative, and integrative abilities. The broad area of assessing civic, intercultural, and ethical capacities languishes even farther behind in terms of test development.[50] Yet we cannot afford to neglect these essential outcomes just because there are no standardized measures to assess them.

Second, standardized tests that stand outside the regular curriculum are, at best, a weak prompt to needed improvement in teaching, learning, and curriculum. Tests can, perhaps, signal a problem, but the test scores themselves do not necessarily point to where or why the problem exists or offer particulars as to solutions. In practice, it takes a combination of valid, reliable instruments and local, grassroots assessments, across a broad array of curricular, pedagogical, and campus activities, to determine the precursors and particulars of academic shortfalls and to determine whether intended interventions are achieving real results.

The right standard for both assessment and accountability at the college level is students' demonstrated ability to apply their learning to complex, unscripted problems in the context of their advanced studies. Far-reaching change is needed to ensure that students work consistently over time on the kinds of higher-order learning—analytical and applied—that prepare them to meet this standard. The best possible way to foster that needed change is to design "milestone" and culminating assessments within the expected curriculum that help students and faculty focus together on the intended level of accomplishment and on what students need to do to improve. These milestone assessments can be designed in ways that check students' intellectual and practical skills as well as their knowledge in a given area. And they can also include dimensions that address social and ethical attentiveness.

Curriculum-embedded assessment, when carefully done, is itself a potential "high-yield" educational reform because, by design, it focuses both faculty and student attention on students' cumulative progress and actual level of attainment. Many campuses already are experimenting with locally designed assignments that show whether students are developing the expected knowledge and skills, and especially, whether they can apply their knowledge to complex problems. This grassroots approach is the most promising way to focus student effort, to engage faculty with evidence about students' cumulative progress, and to inform institutional decisions about needed change.

Standardized tests, administered periodically, can supplement such grassroots approaches. They can, for example, provide useful warning signals when a campus is setting its sights too low. But standardized assessments—especially those that stand outside the curriculum and that rely on a sample of students only—are much too distant from student and faculty attention to serve by themselves as a forceful catalyst for significant educational change.

Recommendation 13

The National Leadership Council recommends that assessments be linked to the essential learning outcomes identified in this report, that assessments be embedded at milestone points in the curriculum—including within students' major fields—and that assessments be made part of the overall graduation requirement.

Students should know from the time they enter college that they will be expected to complete milestone and culminating projects—"authentic performances"—to demonstrate both their progress in relation to the essential outcomes and their ability to use the learning outcomes in the context of their chosen fields. These assessments may consist of portfolios showing a range of student work, or they may center on required student experiences—such as a senior project or supervised student teaching—that are integral to their chosen area of focus. They may include comprehensive examinations in the students' chosen major.

However the assessments are constructed—and this will vary, appropriately, across different fields—the framework for accountabil-

---

THE PRINCIPLES IN PRACTICE

Assess Students' Ability to Apply Learning to Complex Problems

Every student at **Southern Illinois University Edwardsville** completes a senior assignment in the major. The projects vary across different academic fields, but each is designed to ensure that all students have mastered the skills required for their discipline as well as key liberal education outcomes—such as critical thinking, effective writing, and problem solving—that all graduates should possess. Designed by department faculty to "make visible" the learning required for the degree—whether it occurs in the major program or in general education—the capstone projects are assessed using rubrics aligned with the intended learning outcomes and probed for several different kinds of evidence. Individual students receive feedback on their accomplishments while faculty review the assessment evidence at the program level to shape curricular and pedagogical improvements. Over time, the process of collectively designing and scoring senior assignments has encouraged a culture of faculty collaboration.

Assess Students' Ability to Apply Learning to Complex Problems

Carleton College uses writing portfolios to ensure that undergraduates can write competently in a range of styles and contexts. By encouraging students to reflect on—and revise—their writing, the portfolios themselves constitute an important educational experience. To meet the portfolio requirement, students at the end of their sophomore year must submit three to five papers demonstrating their ability to write effectively in different rhetorical and disciplinary contexts; each portfolio must represent at least two of the college's four curricular divisions (Arts and Literature, Humanities, Social Sciences, and Mathematics/Natural Sciences) and must include at least one paper from the "writing requirement" course. Instructors then certify that the papers were written for their classes and indicate if they have since been revised. Finally, students write reflective essays about their writing to introduce the portfolios. Together, the papers must demonstrate mastery of each of several key writing skills—the ability to report on observation, to analyze complex information, to provide interpretation, to use and document sources, and to articulate and support a thesis-driven argument. The writing portfolios have led Carleton faculty to talk about using the portfolios to assess other liberal education outcomes such as quantitative literacy and critical thinking.

ity should be students' demonstrated ability to apply their learning to complex problems. Standards for students' expected level of achievement also will vary by field, but they should all include specific attention to the quality of the students' knowledge, their mastery of key skills, their attentiveness to issues of ethical and social responsibility, and their facility in integrating different parts of their learning.

The National Survey of Student Engagement reports that 60 percent of graduating seniors do some kind of culminating work in college.[51] These culminating activities—whether courses or projects—already are embedded in the expected curriculum; they already are part of the teaching and learning budget. These activities can be structured to show how well students can integrate their knowledge and apply it to complex problems, and students' level of performance on them can be aggregated and made public.

Making students' actual performance the framework for accountability would require, of course, new attention to the 40 percent of college students who do not do culminating work and who earn their degrees by passing the requisite number of courses. But if the intention is to raise the level of students' preparation for twenty-first-century challenges, there is no better place to begin.

Recommendation 14

The National Leadership Council recommends that each campus analyze its assessment findings to ensure that all groups of students are progressing successfully toward the expected learning goals.

This report calls for a new approach to fostering and promoting student success. But in moving toward this needed shift, it is important to attend to lessons already learned with existing metrics of student achievement. Almost everywhere, "college success" is currently documented through reports on enrollment, persistence, degree completion, and sometimes, grades. Probed in more detail, these metrics for success make it indisputably clear that college attainment is stratified by income level, and that there are also significant disparities in attainment between white students and specific groups of racial and ethnic minorities: African Americans, Latinos, and American Indians/Alaskan Natives. Asian American students run the gamut, with some subgroups forging ahead on the traditional measures of success, and others clearly lagging.

As they devise more educationally productive ways of defining and assessing student achievement, educators also need to study closely how different groups of students are progressing within these new standards for success. This will require two levels of analysis. First, each campus can study whether different groups of students are participating equitably in programs and practices—such as first-year experiences, writing-intensive courses, learning communities, and capstone experiences—that have been designed to enrich and strengthen students' academic achievement. On many campuses, such programs disproportionately serve students from more advantaged backgrounds.

By studying the data, campuses can move toward more equitable participation in what they determine to be their most effective educational practices.

Second, as assessments focus more centrally on students' milestone and culminating performances, faculty and staff should also ask whether all groups of students are reaching the expected level of attainment on the essential learning outcomes. By disaggregating emerging data, colleges and universities can hone in on the patterns and likely causes of achievement problems and do a much better job of identifying needed changes in curriculum, teaching quality, academic support, and the larger educational environment.

Recommendation 15

The National Leadership Council recommends that broad-based leadership be developed in order to create campus cultures marked by an unwavering focus on the quality of student learning, by an ethic of continuous improvement, and by structures and rewards that support faculty and staff leadership on these issues.

Faculty and staff on hundreds of campuses are already implementing elements of the Principles of Excellence outlined above. But too often their work touches limited numbers of students or is concentrated in a few areas of the curriculum. Those experimenting with innovative, engaging pedagogical practices are often isolated from one another, unaware that there are kindred spirits just around the corner. Existing reward systems—geared almost exclusively to faculty scholarship and the quality of *individual* teaching—are incompatible with the scope of *collaborative* change and organizational learning that will be needed to raise the quality of all students' educational achievement.

A contemporary framework for educational excellence and its assessment requires new leadership structures and incentives to advance the intended changes. In particular, new organizational practices are needed to both support and reward faculty and staff efforts to foster students' cumulative progress across different parts and levels of the college experience.

Drawing from work by Pat Hutchings and Mary Huber of the Carnegie Foundation for the Advancement of Teaching,[52] we propose that each campus create its own version of a "Teaching and Learning Commons" where faculty, administrators, and student life professionals can come together—across disciplinary lines—to create a culture of shared purposes, to audit the extent to which the educational environment is successfully advancing the expected learning for all groups of students, and to benefit from existing and new efforts to foster student engagement and high achievement.

To foster shared purposes, each campus needs to develop its own vision of the expected learning outcomes (see recommendation 1). By making good use of assessment evidence from many sources, by building widely shared knowledge about successful educational innovations within the community, and by creating a culture of continuous attention to these matters, the Teaching and Learning

Commons can probe the relations between what is intended and what is actually happening. The commons also can serve as a continuing catalyst for effective practices and far-reaching change. In addition, participation in this commons can become an important way of helping new faculty and staff translate the broad aims described in the essential learning outcomes to their particular disciplines and roles. The commons, in short, can play a far-reaching role, creating a culture that consistently "aims high" and that steadfastly focuses—across divisional lines—on campus progress toward making excellence inclusive.

PART 4

A Time for Leadership and Action

★ ★ ★ ★ ★ ★ ★ ★ ★ ★ ★ ★ ★ ★ ★ ★

The educational vision presented here is a call to prepare *all* students for the challenges and complexities of this new global era. The vision builds from a widely shared recognition that in this demanding economic and international environment, almost everyone will need further learning beyond high school, both to expand personal opportunity and to ensure this nation's continuing prosperity.

The LEAP National Leadership Council takes that recognition to a higher level, asking: What kinds of learning? To what ends? Beyond access to college, how should Americans define "success" in college achievement?

In answering these questions, the council urges a strong commitment to provide all students—whatever their choice of institution or career—with a liberal and liberating college education. This report defines liberal education not in terms of specific disciplines studied, but rather as a coherent framework for learning that intentionally fosters, across multiple fields of study, wide-ranging knowledge of science, cultures, and society; high-level intellectual and practical skills; an active commitment to personal and social responsibility; and the demonstrated ability to apply learning to complex problems and challenges.

The council further urges the need for a new compact between educators and American society that focuses simultaneously on essential learning outcomes, effective educational practices, and the integration of learning at increasingly higher levels of accomplishment. The Principles of Excellence articulate this broadly defined educational compact.

Informed by a generation of innovation and scholarly research on effective practices in teaching and learning, the Principles of Excellence offer both challenging standards and flexible guidance for an era of far-reaching educational reform and renewal—in higher education, in the schools, and in the connections between them. And they provide a framework for assessing student learning that both spurs and documents higher levels of student accomplishment.

With campus experimentation already well advanced—on every one of the Principles of Excellence—it is time to move from "pilot efforts" to full-scale commitments. Just as the United States comprehensively transformed designs for learning, at all levels, in the

"With campus experimentation already well advanced—on every one of the Principles of Excellence—it is time to move from 'pilot efforts' to full-scale commitments."

"The Principles of Excellence
describe key steps that every
campus can take to accelerate
the speed and scope of needed
change."

late nineteenth and early twentieth centuries, educators can act now to advance a contemporary set of goals, guiding principles, and practices that will prepare all college students—not just the fortunate few—to reap the full benefits of an engaged and empowering liberal education.

But providing a twenty-first-century education for all college students cannot be done with a few adjustments on the margin. Vigorous and concerted leadership will be needed at many levels to build support for a more contemporary framework for college learning and to accelerate the scope and pace of educational change.

What It Will Take

▶ **Make the Principles of Excellence a Campus Priority**

Colleges, community colleges, and universities stand at the center. Ultimately, it is their role to articulate aims and outcomes for their degrees that both enact their mission and resonate with twenty-first-century realities, to provide rich opportunities for today's diverse students to achieve the essential learning outcomes, and to assure the quality, scope, and level of each student's actual achievement.

Responding to a changing environment, many institutions have already begun to make far-reaching changes, both in defining their core educational purposes and in adopting more engaging and effective educational practices. The vision for twenty-first-century learning presented in these pages reflects and draws on their pioneering leadership and innovation.

But across higher education as a whole, progress in defining robust educational purposes and matching vision with intentional practice has been fragmented at best. The goal now should be to move from partial efforts and islands of innovation to an enterprise-wide focus that embraces the multiple parts of the undergraduate experience. The Principles of Excellence (see p. 26) describe key steps that every campus can take to accelerate the speed and scope of needed change.

▶ **Form Coalitions, across Sectors, for All Students' Long-Term Interests**

While the value of strong educational leadership on each individual campus cannot be overstated, raising the quality of student learning across the board will ultimately require concerted and collective action—between educators and society, and across the various levels of education. Collaborative action is needed because the impediments to educational excellence are systemic rather than isolated. Many high school graduates are underprepared for college, and so higher education is forced to play catch-up. Students need to develop higher-level intellectual and practical skills, but the curriculum in both school and college has been defined, often by state regulation, in terms of course titles and categories, with much too little attention to students' development of important capabilities.

Democracy, global and intercultural learning, active citizenship, and even the skills and knowledge essential to economic innovation remain low priorities at all levels of the educational system because of regulatory and assessment frameworks that largely ignore these crucial areas of learning (see p. 20, fig. 6). Faculty reward systems almost invariably emphasize individual rather than collaborative excellence in both scholarship and teaching, which results in systemic disincentives for faculty members to spend their time in the collaborative redesign of undergraduate education.

The other great systemic impediment to educational reform is the marketplace. When a single college or university independently raises its entrance requirements, or holds students to more rigorous graduation standards in, say, science, mathematics, languages, or global learning, students remain entirely free to take their tuition dollars to another institution that has set less taxing standards. Very few institutions are in a position to stand forth—alone—against these market realities.

For all these reasons, leaders will need to work collectively across institutional boundaries as well as within them to create a market environment that expects educational excellence and that both supports and rewards collaborative work to achieve it.

Many campus leaders already are working at a local level with partner schools to raise the level of college readiness and achievement. But like so much else in the contemporary educational landscape, these are piecemeal, "add-on" efforts that have not yet resulted in far-reaching systemic change. The next step is to move toward collective efforts to broaden public and student understanding about essential learning and to establish higher operative standards across the board for college readiness and college accomplishment. By taking an active role in systemic change efforts at all levels—national, state, and local—colleges and universities can better serve both their students and society, and advance their own institutional interests in educational excellence as well.

▶ **Build Principled and Determined Leadership**

Because the barriers to excellence are systemic, educating American students for today's challenging environment will require proactive and determined leadership as well as coordinated efforts across all parts of American society and all parts of the educational system. While everyone has a role to play in this effort, three forms of enabling leadership will be absolutely essential to champion, support, guide, and reward the hard work of fostering higher levels of achievement across the board: (1) high-profile advocacy from presidents, trustees, school leaders, and employers; (2) curricular leadership from knowledgeable scholars and teachers; and (3) policy leadership at multiple levels to support and reward a new framework for educational excellence.

1. High-profile advocacy from presidents, trustees, school leaders, and employers. Recognized leaders who can command public respect and attention must step forward to explain the value and importance of liberal education—in twenty-first-century terms—both to democ-

"While recognized leaders can make higher achievement a priority, faculty and teachers who work directly with students are the only ones who can make it actually happen."

racy and the economy, and to deploy needed resources to support educational change. Traditionally, presidents, trustees, and school leaders have focused on the needs and priorities of their own institutions. But today, these highly visible and influential leaders need to situate both their public statements and their institutional priorities in a much larger educational context. By using their public pulpits effectively, these influential leaders can build new commitment to a liberating education for all students and new understanding of what will be required to achieve that goal.

Presidents, school leaders, trustees, and leading employers, more than anyone else, are in a position to make the essential learning outcomes a shared national priority and to promote the value of more purposeful connections at all levels of the educational system. And, as campus and school leaders cultivate new public understanding of what matters in college, they can also turn a much-needed spotlight on the public value and significance of their own campus efforts to raise the quality of student accomplishment.

2. Curricular leadership from knowledgeable scholars and teachers. While recognized leaders can make higher achievement a priority, faculty and teachers who work directly with students are the only ones who can make it actually happen.

Scholar-teachers who have standing within the educational community will need to take the lead—in partnerships across school and college—to develop guidelines and curricula that connect rich content with students' progressive mastery of essential skills and competencies. There is already a strong policy interest in creating "seamless alignments" between school and college and in setting higher standards for "college readiness." Building on these existing efforts, faculty and teachers can work together, across the usual school–college dividing lines, to define ascending levels of expected student achievement and to map more purposeful curricular pathways, across different disciplines, that support the expected levels of learning.

Some of this work has already begun, often off the public radar screen. National and state efforts to move from pilot projects to systemic change can draw from countless examples of good practice, in the schools and in higher education. The challenge now is to bring disparate efforts together—nationally, regionally, and locally—around a shared vision for essential learning outcomes that encompasses diverse fields and ascending levels of learning. Equally important, we need to ensure that future teachers and future faculty are well prepared to teach in ways that help students reach a higher level of knowledge and capability.

3. Policy leadership at multiple levels to support and reward a new framework for educational excellence. Leaders in the states, in accreditation agencies, in P–16 initiatives, in educational associations, and on individual campuses have already launched noteworthy (if partial) efforts to foster the learning needed for the twenty-first century. But very few of them have recognized that the Truman-era determination to squeeze all the goals for liberal education into a dozen or so college-level general education courses is an unworkable strategy that now stands in the way of a more productive focus on students' cumulative and integrative learning across the curriculum. Breaking free of this inherited educational cul-de-sac, policy leaders should act together to support faculty and teacher efforts to map the broad aims and outcomes of an empowering liberal education across the entire educational experience, from school through college—including community colleges—and across majors as well as general education. By supporting twenty-first-century expectations for students' cumulative accomplishment and by crafting policies that support and reward needed change, policy leaders can create a far more productive environment for new educational creativity and for the integration of learning at all levels.

▶ Put Employers in Direct Dialogue with Students

Employers have an especially influential role to play in changing student and public understanding about what matters in college. Students already know that a college degree is a passport to expanded economic opportunity. What they need to hear now from their future employers is that narrow learning will limit rather than expand their opportunities. Within their own forums, employers have already championed the value and economic importance of the essential learning outcomes. But students aren't in those forums and many have missed that message entirely.

Employers are already aligned with educators in their recognition that students need an expansive and versatile education rather than narrow training alone. Now, employers—who may also be trustees and regents in both public and private higher education—can join forces with educational leaders to put students in the loop as well. Employers ought to become both visible and audible, explaining on campus Web sites, at career fairs, and even on students' iPods why the essential learning outcomes will prove important beyond college.

Employers already work in tandem with higher education through their campus recruiting efforts, their mentoring and internship programs, their advisory work with faculty and campus programs, and their philanthropic contributions. Employers can use each of these venues to signal their preference for liberal rather than narrow education and the practical value of the essential learning outcomes.

If senior executives, human resources leaders, and campus recruiters insist on the importance of cross-cutting knowledge and versatile intellectual skills, then students will have much stronger incentives to work toward their achievement.

▶ Reclaim the Connection between Liberal Education and Democratic Freedom

Americans are a practical people who understand very well the connection between prosperity and democratic freedom. But as a society, we need to reclaim the insight—well explained by our founders—that freedom is not self-perpetuating. Democracy may be a birthright, but citizens need to be educated about what is involved in sustaining that birthright.

"Students need to hear from their future employers that narrow learning will limit rather than expand their opportunities."

The first lesson in that education should be new clarity about the root meaning of *liber*, the Latin word for a free person. In American society, liberal education has evolved as the kind of education necessary to a free people: to self-governance and democracy. But liberal education has never lived up to the full promise of democracy because this society has never before attempted to provide a liberating education for all Americans.

Moving forward in this new global century, we have a historic opportunity to redeem that promise by making educational excellence newly inclusive. The essential learning outcomes described in these pages are important to the economy, certainly. But they are even more important to American democracy. As Americans mobilize determined leadership for educational reform—from presidents, trustees, school leaders, faculty, teachers, staff, employers, policy makers, and everyone else—we need to put the future of democracy at the center of our efforts.

An educational program that is indifferent to democracy will ultimately deplete it. But a democracy united around a shared commitment to excellence for everyone is this nation's best investment in our shared future.

Liberal Education and America's Promise

While college has become a gateway to opportunity in American society, it is not a magic carpet. Ultimately, it is the quality of learning, not the possession of a diploma, that will make all the difference—to individuals, to an economy dependent upon innovation, and to the integrity of the democracy we create together.

The proposals offered here build on the historic strengths of higher education in the United States, especially the academy's commitment to inclusion and excellence, its sense of responsibility to the larger society, its embrace of democratic principles and values, and its record of achievement in advancing innovative solutions to important problems.

With this report, the LEAP National Leadership Council urges a comprehensive commitment, not just to prepare all students for college, but to provide the most powerful forms of learning for all who enroll in college.

Working together, with determination, creativity, and a larger sense of shared purpose, Americans can fulfill the promise of a liberating college education—for every student and for America's future.

What Individual Colleges, Community Colleges, and Universities Can Do

★ ★ ★ ★ ★ ★ ★ ★ ★ ★ ★ ★ ★ ★ ★ ★ ★ ★

✴ Vision

The institution—through dialogue with the wider community—articulates a vision for student accomplishment that addresses the essential learning outcomes and the Principles of Excellence in ways appropriate to mission, students, and educational programs.

✴ Resources

Campus leaders—including presidents, trustees, and senior leaders—advance this vision through their strategic planning, fundraising, resource allocation, and staffing.

✴ Integrative Learning

The institution creates an intellectual commons where faculty and staff work together to connect the essential outcomes with the content and practices of their educational programs, including general education, departmental majors, the cocurriculum, and assessments.

✴ Intentional Students

The institution teaches students how to integrate the essential learning outcomes within a purposeful, coherent, and carefully sequenced plan of study.

✴ Accomplishment

Faculty and staff work to develop student knowledge and capabilities cumulatively and sequentially, drawing on all types of courses—from general education and the majors to electives—as well as non-course experiences.

✴ Evidence

Faculty and staff members work together—across courses and programs—to assess students' cumulative progress, to audit the connections between intended learning and student accomplishment, to share findings about effective educational practices, and to advance needed change.

✴ Recognition

Faculty and staff reward systems are organized to support collaborative work—"our work"—as well as individual excellence, and to foster a culture of shared focus and collaborative inquiry about students' progress and cumulative learning across the multiple parts of the college experience.

LEAP

APPENDIX A

A Guide to Effective Educational Practices

The following teaching and learning practices have been widely tested and have shown benefits for college students, especially those from historically underserved backgrounds.[53] Because they feature various forms of active learning, these innovative educational practices also are especially well suited for assessing students' cumulative learning. However, on almost all campuses, these practices remain optional rather than essential.

First-Year Seminars and Experiences

Many schools now build into the curriculum first-year seminars or other programs that bring small groups of students together with faculty or staff on a regular basis. Typically, first-year experiences place a strong emphasis on critical inquiry, frequent writing, information literacy, collaborative learning, and other skills that develop students' intellectual and practical competencies. First-year seminars can involve students with cutting-edge questions in scholarship and with faculty members' own research.

Common Intellectual Experiences

The older idea of a "core" curriculum has evolved into a variety of modern forms such as a set of required common courses, or a vertically organized general education program that includes advanced integrative studies and/or required participation in a learning community (see below). These programs often combine broad themes—e.g., technology and society, or global interdependence—with a variety of curricular and cocurricular options for students.

Learning Communities

The key goals for learning communities are to encourage integration of learning across courses and to involve students with "big questions" that matter beyond the classroom. Students take two or more linked courses as a group and work closely with one another and with their professors. Many learning communities explore a common topic and/or common readings through the lenses of different disciplines. Some deliberately link "liberal arts" and "professional courses"; others feature service learning (see below).

Writing-Intensive Courses

These courses emphasize writing at all levels of instruction and across the curriculum, including final-year projects. Students are encouraged to produce and revise various forms of writing for different audiences in different disciplines. The effectiveness of this repeated practice "across the curriculum" has led to parallel efforts in such areas as quantitative reasoning, oral communication, information literacy, and on some campuses, ethical inquiry.

Collaborative Assignments and Projects

Collaborative learning combines two key goals: learning to work and solve problems in the company of others, and sharpening one's own understanding by listening seriously to the insights of others, especially those with different backgrounds and life experiences. Approaches range from forming study groups within a course, to team-based assignments and writing, to cooperative projects and research.

"Science as Science Is Done"/Undergraduate Research

With strong support from the National Science Foundation and the research community, scientists are reshaping their courses to connect key concepts and questions with students' early and active involvement in systematic investigation and research. The goal is to involve students with actively contested questions, empirical observation, cutting-edge technologies, and the sense of excitement that comes from working to answer important questions. These reforms are part of a broader movement to provide research experiences for students in all disciplines.

Diversity/Global Learning

Many colleges and universities now emphasize courses and programs that help students explore cultures, life experiences, and worldviews different from their own. These studies—which may address U.S. diversity, world cultures, or both—often explore "difficult differences" such as racial, ethnic, and gender inequality, or continuing struggles around the globe for human rights, freedom, and power. Frequently, intercultural studies are augmented by experiential learning in the community and/or by study abroad.

Service Learning, Community-Based Learning

In these programs, field-based "experiential learning" with community partners is an instructional strategy—and often a required part of the course. The idea is to give students direct experience with issues they are studying in the curriculum and with ongoing efforts to analyze and solve problems in the community. These programs model the idea that giving something back to the community is an important college outcome, and that working with community partners is good preparation for citizenship, work, and life.

Internships

Internships are another increasingly common form of experiential learning. The idea is to provide students with direct experience in a work setting—usually related to their career interests—and to give them the benefit of supervision and coaching from professionals in the field. If the internship is taken for "course credit," students complete a project or paper that is approved by a faculty member.

Capstone Courses and Projects

Whether they're called "senior capstones" or some other name, these culminating experiences require students nearing the end of their college years to create a project of some sort that integrates and applies what they've learned. The project might be a research paper, a performance, a portfolio of "best work," or an exhibit of artwork. Capstones are offered both in departmental programs and, increasingly, in general education as well.

APPENDIX B
A Note on Commercial Colleges

Although only about 5 percent of students attend for-profit or commercial colleges and universities, these types of schools make up 47 percent of the postsecondary institutions in the United States.[54] Much like businesses, these colleges can be bought and sold, and their profits—which are about 15 percent[55]—are taxed like those of other profit-making entities. Most for-profits operate at less than $50 million a year, though a few notable names have revenues of more than $100 million: Kaplan; University of Phoenix's parent company, the Apollo Group; and about ten other such companies. There are more than four thousand commercial colleges in the United States.

About half of the students enrolled in commercial colleges come from minority communities. Many are adults who did not begin a bachelor's program immediately after high school. As Guilbert Hentschke from the Rossier School of Education at the University of Southern California observes, because they "are motivated more by the market than by academics, for-profits are likely to focus on the programs for employment sectors with high demand. . . . The traditional liberal arts education is not on the menu."

The number of for-profit colleges has grown very rapidly—particularly from 1990 to 2000, when there was a more than 100 percent increase in for-profit campuses. And from 1995 to 2000, enrollment increased by 52 percent. Much of this growth can be attributed to the largest of the for-profits, but all these schools are growing, in part as a result of the "short-cycle" degrees they offer and the strong focus on job placement after graduation.

Because of this focus on job placement, much of the curriculum at for-profit institutions is driven by how "in-demand" a given employment sector or job is at that time. Most commercial colleges, as a result, offer a relatively small number of programs that give students specific skills for a predetermined career choice.

The average cost of attendance at commercial colleges is relatively high compared to public two-year and four-year institutions. One source of funding is the Pell Grant program, which provides need-based grants to low-income students. In 2000–2001, 1,918 for-profit institutions participated in the Pell Grant program, comprising approximately 35 percent of the total number of participating institutions. In the same year, for-profit institutions received 14 percent of the total Pell Grant funds available to low-income students,[56] while enrolling about 5 percent of students in the United States.

In 2003–4, students in commercial colleges in New York State made up 4.3 percent of all college students, but received about 25 percent of federal and state tuition assistance grants and about half of federally guaranteed student loans.[57]

COMMENTARY

"Proprietary colleges often do not require much general education. In fact, they often promote themselves by emphasizing that students do not have to take courses in the social sciences or humanities. The institutions may require applied communications and mathematics courses, but the operative word is 'applied.'"

—Kent A. Farnsworth, former president of Crowder College; professor of community college leadership studies and director of the Center for International Community College Education and Leadership, University of Missouri–St. Louis.

Notes

1. The Education Trust–West, *The High School Diploma: Making It More Than an Empty Promise* (Oakland, CA: The Education Trust–West, 2002), 5.

2. National Center for Education Statistics, *The Condition of Education* (Washington, DC: U.S. Department of Education, 2006), 66.

3. Horatio Alger Association of Distinguished Americans, *The State of Our Nation's Youth*, 2005–2006 (Alexandria, VA: Horatio Alger Association of Distinguished Americans, 2005), 17.

4. Clifford Adelman, "The Propaganda of Numbers," *The Chronicle of Higher Education*, October 13, 2006. Adelman takes issue with the widely publicized figure that shows bachelor's and associate's degree attainment—ten years after beginning high school—languishing at 18 percent. Adelman points to the congruence between figures from the U.S. Census Bureau and the findings from a longitudinal study of eighth graders' transcripts from 1988 through 2000 conducted by the National Center for Education Statistics, which shows that 35 percent of that student cohort had attained either a bachelor's degree or an associate's degree by 2000, with 28 or 29 percent holding bachelor's degrees. See also U.S. Census Bureau, Current Population Survey, 2006 Annual Social and Economic Supplement.

5. By age twenty-four, 75 percent of students from the top income quartile receive bachelor's degrees, while less than 9 percent of those from the bottom quartile do so. "Family Income and Higher Education Opportunity 1970 to 2003," *Postsecondary Education Opportunity*, no. 156 (2005). For racial disparities in degree attainment, see U.S. Department of Education, National Center for Education Statistics, *Condition of Education Statistics 2006* (Washington, DC: U.S. Government Printing Office, 2006), Table 31-3. For an overall analysis, see Kati Haycock, *Promise Abandoned: How Policy Choices and Institutional Practices Restrict College Opportunities* (Washington, DC: The Education Trust, 2006).

6. In September 2005, U.S. Secretary of Education Margaret Spellings announced the formation of the Secretary of Education's Commission on the Future of Higher Education and charged it with developing a comprehensive national strategy for postsecondary education. In September 2006, the commission issued its report, *A Test of Leadership: Charting the Future of U.S. Higher Education* (Washington, DC: U.S. Department of Education, 2006).

7. Derek Bok, *Our Underachieving Colleges* (Princeton, NJ: Princeton University Press, 2006).

8. Clifford Adelman, "'Global Preparedness' of Pre-9/11 College Graduates: What the U.S. Longitudinal Studies Say," *Tertiary Education and Management* 10 (2004): 243–60.

9. The Conference Board, the Partnership for 21st Century Skills, Corporate Voices for Working Families, and the Society for Human Resource Management, *Are They Really Ready to Work? Employers' Perspectives on the Basic Knowledge and Applied Skills of New Entrants to the 21st Century U.S. Workforce* (New York: The Conference Board, 2006).

10. See, for example, Building Engineering and Science Talent, *The Talent Imperative: Meeting America's Challenge in Science and Engineering ASAP* (San Diego, CA: BEST, 2003); Committee on Prospering in the Global Economy of the 21st Century: An Agenda for American Science and Technology, National Academy of Sciences, National Academy of Engineering, Institute of Medicine, *Rising above the Gathering Storm: Energizing and Employing America for a Brighter Economic Future* (Washington, DC: The National Academies Press, 2006); Council on Competitiveness, *Innovate America: Thriving in a World of*

Challenge and Change (Washington, DC: Council on Competitiveness, 2005); and Duke University, *Framing the Engineering Outsourcing Debate: Placing the United States on a Level Playing Field with China and India* (Durham, NC: Duke University, 2005).

11. The more rigorous the high school curriculum taken, the more likely students are to enroll in a four-year institution and ultimately achieve a bachelor's degree. Clifford Adelman, *The Toolbox Revisited: Paths to Degree Completion from High School Through College* (Washington, DC: U.S. Department of Education, 2006). But many students do not take a strong college preparatory curriculum in high school. Probing this issue in more detail, scholars at the National Center for Educational Statistics identified three levels of high school curriculum taken by students enrolling directly in a four-year college or university in 1995–96. The three levels of study included (1) *Core Curriculum and Below:* four years of English, three years of mathematics, three years of science, and three years of social studies—one third of the study group took this or less; (2) *Mid-Level:* includes all components of the Core but expands to include Algebra I and geometry, at least one year of a foreign language, and at least two of the science courses chosen from biology, chemistry, or physics—taken by half the students; (3) *Rigorous Curriculum:* includes all components of Mid-Level, a fourth year of mathematics (including precalculus or higher), biology, chemistry, and physics, and at least one Advanced Placement course—taken by 19 percent. Three years after enrolling in college, 79 percent of those who took the Rigorous Curriculum were continuously enrolled in their initial institutions, compared with 55 percent of those who took the Core Curriculum and 62 percent of those who took the Mid-Level. High school course-taking patterns were stratified by income and by racial/ethnic background, but completing a rigorous curriculum predicted college success even with controls for background. The study did not include community college students. Laura J. Horn and Lawrence K. Kojaku, *High School Academic Curriculum and the Persistence Path through College: Persistence and Transfer Behavior of Undergraduates 3 Years After Entering 4-Year Institutions* (Washington, DC: U.S. Department of Education, National Center for Education Statistics, 2001).

12. Peter D. Hart Research Associates, *Key Findings from Focus Groups among College Students and College-Bound High School Students* (Washington, DC: Peter D. Hart Research Associates, 2004), 6. This research was conducted for the LEAP initiative.

13. Ellen M. Bradburn, Rachael Berger, Xiaojie Li, Katharin Peter, and Kathryn Rooney, *A Descriptive Summary of 1999–2000 Bachelor's Degree Recipients 1 Year Later, With an Analysis of Time to Degree* (Washington, DC: U.S. Department of Education, National Center for Education Statistics, 2003).

14. Laura Horn and Stephanie Nevill, *Profile of Undergraduates in U.S. Postsecondary Institutions: 2003–2004* (Washington, DC: U.S. Department of Education, National Center for Education Statistics, 2006), 87, table 3.3.

15. Research on the benefits of active and engaged learning is voluminous. Engagement as a "key to student success" is summarized and grounded in campus case studies in George D. Kuh, Jillian Kinzie, John H. Schuh, Elizabeth J. Whitt, and Associates, *Student Success in College: Creating Conditions That Matter* (San Francisco, CA: Jossey-Bass, 2005). Results of a study testing the active learning findings in liberal arts education are reported by Ernest T. Pascarella, Gregory C. Wolniak, Tricia A. D. Seifert, Ty M. Cruce, and Charles F. Blaich in *Liberal Arts Colleges and Liberal Arts Education: New Evidence on Impacts*, ASHE Higher Education Report vol. 31, no. 3 (San Francisco, CA: Jossey–Bass, 2005). See also Ernest T. Pascarella and Patrick T. Terenzini, *How College Affects Students, Volume 2, A Third Decade of Research* (San Francisco, CA: Jossey-Bass, 2005). For research on the benefits of specific educational practices, see note 53.

16. George D. Kuh, Jillian Kinzie, Ty Cruce, Rick Shoup, and Robert M. Gonyea, "Connecting the Dots: Multi-Faceted Analyses of the Relationships Between Student Engagement Results from the NSSE, and the Institutional Practices and Conditions that Foster Student Success" (Indiana University, Bloomington, 2006); Kenneth I. Maton and Freeman A. Hrabowski III, "Increasing the Number of African American PhDs in the Sciences and Engineering: A Strengths-Based Approach," *American Psychologist* 59, no. 6 (2004), 547–56. For an analysis of the extent of minority and low-income student participation, see Kathleen M. Goodman, Tricia A. Seifert, James D. Jorgensen, Ernest T. Pascarella, Gregory C. Wolniak, Charles F. Blaich, and Carol Geary Schneider, "How Do Race and Socioeconomic Background Influence Experiences of Good Practices in Undergraduate Education?" (Paper presented at the Association for the Study of Higher Education Annual Conference, Anaheim, CA, November 4, 2006).

17. President's Commission on Higher Education, *Higher Education for American Democracy: A Report of the President's Commission on Higher Education* (Washington, DC: U.S. Government Printing Office, 1947), 49.

18. Peter D. Hart Research Associates, *Report of Findings Based on Focus Groups among Business Executives* (Washington, DC: Peter D. Hart Research Associates, 2006); Peter D. Hart Research Associates, *Key Findings from Focus Groups among College Students and College-Bound High School Students* (Washington, DC: Peter D. Hart Research Associates, 2004). Both studies were conducted for the LEAP initiative. Focus group participants produced their own written definitions of the term "liberal education" prior to discussion of the topic.

19. "The Bureau of Labor Statistics . . . reports that even those born at the tail end of the baby boom held an average of 10.2 jobs between ages 18 and 38, from 1978 to 2002. A 2004 study by the Families and Work Institute, a nonprofit research group, polled Generation Y employees and found they were significantly more likely to leave their jobs than employees who were their comparable ages in 1977—70 percent, compared with 52 percent." Anna Bahney, "A Life Between Jobs," *New York Times*, June 8, 2006.

20. Roberts T. Jones, "Liberal Education for the Twenty-first Century: Business Expectations," *Liberal Education* 91, no. 2 (2005): 32–37.

21. Norman R. Augustine, "Learning to Lose? Our Education System Isn't Ready for a World of Competition," *Washington Post*, December 6, 2005.

22. Business–Higher Education Forum, *Spanning the Chasm: A Blueprint for Action* (Washington, DC: Business–Higher Education Forum, 1999), 7.

23. Peter D. Hart Research Associates, *Report of Findings Based on Focus Groups among Business Executives* (Washington, DC: Peter D. Hart Research Associates, 2006), 1.

24. Keith Peden, personal communication, 2006.

25. This point was made repeatedly by employers participating in focus groups convened for the LEAP initiative and also in the more than two dozen campus–community dialogues about goals for college learning that were convened by AAC&U and partner colleges and universities between fall 2002 and 2004.

26. Steven Brint, Mark Riddle, Lori Turk-Bicakci, and Charles S. Levy, "From the Liberal to the Practical Arts in American Colleges and Universities: Organizational Analysis and Curricular Change," *The Journal of Higher Education* 76, no. 2 (2005): 151–80. Reflecting the twentieth-century division of higher learning into liberal arts versus professional categories, analyses of liberal education usually take as a proxy the percentage of graduates who major in one of the arts and sciences disciplines and/or the percentage of students who attend institutions that offer an arts and sciences curriculum primarily. Using the former template, this study reviews American college students' relative preference from 1915 to 2000 for "liberal arts" versus the occupational–professional majors. The study shows that, over the course of the century, majoring in the

liberal arts and sciences became increasingly concentrated in the "selective baccalaureate-granting institutions and other institutions with strong academic profiles, as measured by average SAT/ACT scores." What was originally a functional divide between different kinds of learning "*has become largely a status divide*" (emphasis added). Institutions enrolling students with lower test scores and family income generally emphasize occupational–professional studies. The longitudinal analysis shows that the arts and sciences fields began to slip from their dominant position in terms of degrees granted just before the Great Depression, then regained lost ground in the 1960s, rising to 55 percent of degrees granted, before slipping back again. In recent years, about 58 percent of baccalaureate degrees have been awarded in occupational–professional programs.

27. ABET Engineering Accreditation Commission, *Criteria for Accrediting Engineering Programs* (Baltimore, MD: 2004). ABET, which accredits nearly two thousand engineering programs at more than 350 institutions, adopted an outcomes-based strategy for accreditation in 1996, with the publication of *Engineering Criteria 2000*.

28. "Among public high schools that year [2002–3], NCES [National Center for Education Statistics] estimated enrollments at 1.2 million for dual credit courses, 1.8 million for AP courses, and 165,000 for IB courses." The Western Interstate Commission for Higher Education, *Accelerated Learning Options: Moving the Needle on Access and Success* (Boulder, CO: Western Interstate Commission for Higher Education, 2006), 2.

29. Clifford Adelman, *Principal Indicators of Student Academic Histories in Postsecondary Education, 1972–2000* (Washington, DC: Institute for Education Sciences, U.S. Department of Education, 2004), 87.

30. See note 8 above and figure 1 on page 8.

31. Jon D. Miller, "Civic Scientific Literacy: A Necessity in the 21st Century," *FAS Public Interest Report* 55, no. 1 (2002): 3–6. A political scientist at Northwestern University, Miller has devised a measure of "civic scientific literacy" that includes three dimensions: (1) an understanding of basic scientific concepts and constructs, such as the molecule, DNA, and the structure of the solar system; (2) an understanding of the nature and process of scientific inquiry; and (3) a pattern of regular information consumption about scientific topics and developments. By 1999, studies using these measures concluded that approximately 17 percent of Americans demonstrate scientific literacy at this "civic" level, up from 10 percent a decade earlier. The strongest predictor of civic scientific literacy is the number of college-level science courses taken.

32. See note 10.

33. Peter D. Hart Research Associates, *Key Findings from Focus Groups among College Students and College-Bound High School Students* (Washington, DC: Peter D. Hart Research Associates, 2004).

34. Martha Nussbaum, *Cultivating Humanity: A Classical Defense of Reform in Liberal Education* (Cambridge, MA: Harvard University Press, 1998).

35. Azar Nafisi, "The Republic of the Imagination," *Washington Post*, December 5, 2004.

36. National Center for Education Statistics, *Integrated Postsecondary Education Data System* (Washington, DC: U.S. Department of Education, 2005), table 213.

37. National Center for Education Statistics, *First-Generation Students in Postsecondary Education: A Look at Their College Transcripts.* (Washington, DC: U.S. Department of Education, 2005).

38. See note 13.

39. U.S. Department of Education, National Center for Education Statistics,

Beginning Postsecondary Students Longitudinal Study Data Analysis System (Washington, DC: U.S. Government Printing Office). For beginning students of all ages, 45.4 percent start at community colleges and 4.5 percent at other two-year schools. For beginning students twenty years old and younger, 40.9 percent start at community colleges and 3.4 percent at other two-year schools.

40. John D. Bransford, Ann L. Brown, and Rodney R. Cocking, eds., *How People Learn: Brain, Mind, Experience, and School* (Washington, DC: National Academies Press, 1999).

41. See note 28.

42. "Over 90 percent of college students age 19 at the beginning of the 2000–01 school year worked at an employee job at some time during that academic year and following summer, with the vast majority working during both the school year and the summer." National Longitudinal Survey of Youth, www.bls.gov/nls.

43. Lee S. Shulman, "Pedagogies of Uncertainty," *Liberal Education* 91, no. 2 (2005): 18–25.

44. Jack Meacham and Jerry G. Gaff, "Learning Goals in Mission Statements: Implications for Educational Leadership," *Liberal Education* 92, no. 1 (2006): 6–13.

45. On the effects of service learning, see Alexander Astin, "Liberal Education and Democracy: The Case for Pragmatism," in *Education and Democracy: Re-imagining Liberal Learning in America*, ed. Robert Orrill (New York: College Board, 1997); Maryann Jacobi Gray, et al. *Combining Service and Learning in Higher Education: Evaluation of the Learn and Serve America, Higher Education Program* (New York: The RAND Corporation, 1999). On the effects of diversity experiences, see Angelo N. Ancheta and Christopher F. Edley, Jr., "Brief of the American Educational Research Association, the Association of American Colleges and Universities, and the American Association for Higher Education as *Amici Curiae* in Support of Respondents," in *Grutter v. Bollinger* (Washington, DC: United States Supreme Court, 2003). On the effects of diversity learning and civic engagement, see Patricia Gurin, Eric L. Dey, Sylvia Hurtado, and Gerald Gurin, "Diversity and Higher Education: Theory and Impact on Educational Outcomes," *Harvard Educational Review* 72 (2002): 330–67.

46. Association of American Colleges and Universities, *Liberal Education Outcomes: A Preliminary Report on Achievement in College* (Washington, DC: Association of American Colleges and Universities, 2005), 5.

47. Norman Nie and Sunshine Hillygus, "Education and Democratic Citizenship," in *Making Good Citizens: Education and Civil Society*, Diane Ravitch and Joseph Viteritti, eds. (New Haven, CT: Yale University Press, 2001).

48. U.S. Department of Education, *A Test of Leadership: Charting the Future of U.S. Higher Education* (Washington, DC: U.S. Department of Education, 2006).

49. Lee S. Shulman, "Principles for the Uses of Assessment in Policy and Practice: President's Report to the Board of Trustees of the Carnegie Foundation for the Advancement of Teaching," 2006, www.teaglefoundation.org/learning/pdf/2006_shulman_assessment.pdf.

50. Richard J. Shavelson, *Student Learning Assessment: From History to an Audacious Proposal* (Washington, DC: Association of American Colleges and Universities, forthcoming).

51. National Survey of Student Engagement, *Exploring Different Dimensions of Student Engagement: 2005 Annual Survey Results* (Bloomington, IN: Indiana University Center for Postsecondary Research, 2005).

52. Mary Taylor Huber and Pat Hutchings, *The Advancement of Learning: Building the Teaching Commons* (San Francisco, CA: Jossey-Bass, 2005).

53. An extensive literature has established the value for students of active, en-

gaged, and collaborative forms of learning. The effective educational practices
described in appendix A reflect more than two decades of work on campus
to translate these broad research findings into curriculum and pedagogy.
The recommended practices, while not exhaustive, provide a "cornerstone to
capstone" framing that potentially fosters active intellectual engagement and
practice across the entire educational experience. Research findings on the benefits of first-year experiences, learning communities, diversity learning, service
learning, undergraduate research, and collaborative/cooperative learning are
summarized in Ernest T. Pascarella and Patrick T. Terenzini, *How College Affects
Students, Volume 2, A Third Decade of Research* (San Francisco, CA: Jossey-
Bass, 2005). For the value of a common intellectual experience in general
education, see Alexander W. Astin, *What Matters in College? Four Critical Years
Revisited* (San Francisco, CA: Jossey-Bass, 1993), 331–32, 424–28. For the value
of writing-intensive courses, see Richard J. Light, *Making the Most of
College: Students Speak Their Minds* (Cambridge, MA: Harvard University
Press, 2001), 54–62; Derek Bok, *Our Underachieving Colleges* (Princeton, NJ:
Princeton University Press, 2006), 82–101. For experiential learning, see John
D. Bransford, Ann. L. Brown, and Rodney R. Cocking, eds., *How People Learn:
Brain, Mind, Experience and School* (Washington, DC: National Academies
Press, 1999); K. Patricia Cross, *Learning Is About Making Connections, The
Cross Papers, Number 3* (Phoenix, AZ: League for Innovation in the Community
Colleges, June, 1999). For "science as science is done," see Judith A. Ramaley
and Rosemary R. Haggett, "Engaged and Engaging Science: A Component of a
Good Liberal Education, *Peer Review* 7, no. 2 (2005), 8–12; Eugenia Etkina, Jose
P. Mestre, and Angela M. O'Donnell, "The Impact of the Cognitive Revolution on
Science Learning and Teaching," in *The Cognitive Revolution in Educational
Psychology*, James M. Royer, ed. (Greenwich, CT: Information Age, 2005),
119–64. While the research on capstone experiences is scant, Pascarella and
Terenzini report that "[intellectual development] is stimulated by academic
experiences that purposefully provide for . . . integration." *How College Affects
Students: Findings and Insights from Twenty Years of Research* (San Francisco,
CA: Jossey-Bass, 1991), 619. See also *How College Affects Students, Volume 2,
A Third Decade of Research*, 608. For two influential summaries that helped to
accelerate campus-based work on engaged and active learning and its assess-
ment, see Study Group on the Conditions of Excellence in American Higher
Education, *Involvement in Learning* (Washington, DC: U.S. Department of
Education, 1984); Arthur W. Chickering and Zelda F. Gamson, eds., *Applying the
Seven Principles for Good Practice in Undergraduate Education*, New Directions
for Teaching and Learning, no. 47 (San Francisco, CA: Jossey-Bass, 1991). The
National Study of Student Engagement provides a set of metrics that enables a
campus to indicate the extent to which its students are participating in various
forms of active practice, such as extensive writing, integrative learning
assignments, and capstone/culminating projects.

54. Unless otherwise noted, all data presented in the appendix are drawn from
Guilbert C. Hentschke, "U.S. For-Profit Postsecondary Institutions—Departure or
Extension?" *International Higher Education* no. 35 (Spring 2004): 15–16.

55. Blumenstyk, Goldie, "Why For-Profit Colleges Are Like Health Clubs," *Chronicle
of Higher Education*, May 5, 2006.

56. Jacqueline E. King, *2003 Status Report on the Pell Grant Program* (Washington,
DC: American Council on Education Center for Policy Analysis, 2003), 9.

57. Karen Arensen, "Report Calls for Tighter Rules on Profit-Making Colleges,"
New York Times, May 22, 2006.